FLY FISHING
Saltwater Basics

C. Boyd Pfeiffer

Illustrated by Dave Hall

D0839485

STACKPOLE
BOOKS

0 11557 02763 1

Dedication

*To the memory of my dear wife, Jackie, who always was
and always will be the inspiration for everything I have done,
everything I do, and everything I might accomplish.*

Copyright © 1999 by C. Boyd Pfeiffer

Published by
STACKPOLE BOOKS
5067 Ritter Road
Mechanicsburg, PA 17055
www.stackpolebooks.com

Printed in the United States

First edition

10 9 8 7 6 5 4 3 2 1

Cover design by Caroline Stover
Cover drawings by Dave Hall

Library of Congress Cataloging-in-Publication Data

Pfeiffer, C. Boyd
    Fly Fishing Saltwater Basics / C. Boyd Pfeiffer.
        p.   cm.
    Includes bibliographical references.
    ISBN 0-8117-2763-7 (pbk.)
    1. Saltwater fly fishing. I. Title.
    SH456.2.P44   1999
    799. 1'6—dc21   99-14048
                                                     CIP

Contents

Acknowledgments

Books might be written by one or a few authors, but they are usually a culmination of help from others, including their experiences, theories, experiments, comments, suggestions, and thoughts, and often assimilate ideas from other books and writers. That is certainly true of this book, with special appreciation to all those—close longtime friends and one-time acquaintances—with whom I have fished over the years and in the process learned, developed, and had fun. To all, my thanks. Special thanks are due my longtime fishing partner and close friend Chuck Edghill for his careful reading of the manuscript and for all his suggestions and corrections. His help much improved this book, although any omissions, mistakes, or other failings are ultimately mine.

Introduction

Think of saltwater fly fishing, and many of us immediately conjure up visions of tropical flats, leaping tarpon shaking water like a wet sheepdog, stealthy bonefish zigzagging across the flats, toothy barracuda lurking on the edge of channels, or snook hiding in the shade of a twisted mangrove.

That's an important and exciting part of saltwater fly fishing, but the sport is much broader, involving almost all saltwater species and available to almost everyone everywhere. There is excellent fly fishing all along the Atlantic coast for stripers, bluefish, redfish, perch, little tunny, and shad. On the Gulf you can find redfish, trout, cobia, snook, seatrout, and albacore. When working Pacific waters, catches might be Pacific barracuda, rockfish, roosterfish, calico bass, stripers, shad, or salmon. And those are just a few of the coastal species. Off all coasts there are tuna, dolphin, sharks, billfish, wahoo, and mackerel.

Saltwater fly fishing might be thought of as the last frontier for the fly rodder, but your first immersion in it does not require a change of tackle

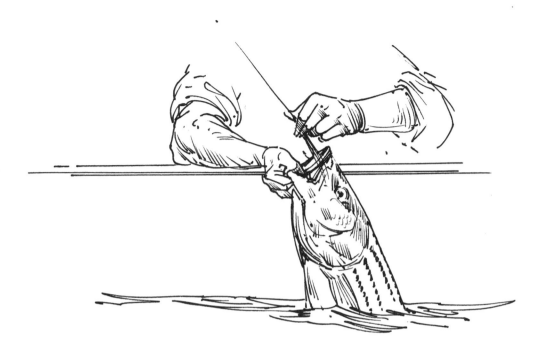

from your trout or bass gear, nor extensive knowledge of a new species and how to fish for it. Exciting fishing is available everywhere by targeting easy fish for starters—fish you may already be familiar with on other tackle.

Statistics show that 50 percent of the population lives within 50 miles of the coast. That, and a fine interstate road system makes coastal forays easier than ever. And many anglers—regardless of their distance from the salt—are increasingly saltwater fly fishing, or starting to try it.

Since all families like to visit the beach and ocean, it is easy to include fishing with a family vacation, summer outing, or extended travel trip. With plentiful catches under some, though not all, conditions, it's an easy way to introduce the rest of your family to fly fishing.

There are many advantages to saltwater fly fishing. You can combine it with other fishing, should you also like to cast with spinning or casting tackle or troll. Keep a rigged fly rod for those occasions when the fishing is so good that you want to fling a fly into breaking fish or when you get tired of other fishing and want to give fly rodding a try. Use it as little or as much as you like as an alternative to fishing with other gear.

You can fish for smaller quarry, such as calico bass on the west coast, small trout on the Gulf, or white perch in the Atlantic, or gear up to go after big game such as billfish and sharks. You can fish mangrove-laced shorelines, rocky northeast coasts, steep Pacific shoreline cliffs, sandy beaches, skinny flats, offshore blue water, inshore structure such as jetties and piers, current, rips, tide lines, marshy shorelines, inlets, bays, tidal rivers, creeks, low tides, high tides, running tides, under screaming birds, over breaking bait, to schooling fish, at individual fish, blind fishing, night fishing, and sight fishing. There is no end to the variety of saltwater angling and the new thrills that come each day when on salt water with fly rod in hand. With the variety of fish and conditions available, you can make it the sport you want, and you can make it different each day, fishing for different species in different areas. If variety is the spice of life, then fly fishing is the epitome of saltwater angling—perhaps any angling.

Chapter 1

Tackle

Saltwater fly fishing requires the same tackle used in fresh water, with some important considerations. Saltwater fly fishing is rough on tackle. The fish are usually larger and tougher than freshwater species and fight harder and longer. Salt air and water are corrosive to tackle. Choose an outfit with noncorrosive parts that will hold up to tough fishing conditions. Anodized aluminum, stainless steel, or nonrusting parts are a must. The reel must have sufficient line and backing capacity for long runs, and the rod must have the power for long casts and a determined end fight.

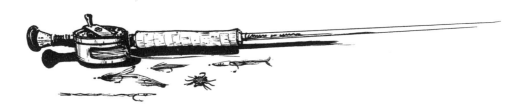

Lines for highly specialized fishing include those with controlled limpness for tropical or cold-weather fishing, special tapers for large flies and long casts, and extrafast-sinking lines for getting deep. Flies must be durable and tied on noncorrosive hooks.

Once you get into saltwater fly fishing, you quickly realize that you need several different outfits. Tackle for white perch is far different from that needed for white marlin on the same Atlantic coast. "Light" and "heavy" tackle are subjective terms. A 12-weight outfit is very light for billfish but heavily overgunned for most inshore fish.

In some circles, light-tackle fishing is popular. This involves using fly tackle that is on the cutting edge of light for a particular species or size of fish. It can be dangerous and is often unsporting and unfair to the fish. The danger comes with fighting a fish to the limits of the rod, which might splinter and break. It also can tie up the boat or other anglers, as light tackle requires more time to land a fish. The main problem with a long fight is that fish build up lactic acid in their muscles, stressing them severely and often causing death. You might release them alive, but they can die hours later. Exhausted, stressed fish are also easy targets for sharks. Though light-tackle fishing can be fun as an occasional stunt and to test your fish-handling skills, it's better to use tackle suitable for the size and species, fight the fish fairly to prevent exhaustion, and release it properly and promptly.

Small fish up to a couple pounds require only light rods, a direct-drive reel, and minimal backing—perhaps no more than 50 yards plus the fly line. A 6-weight outfit is typical here. Medium fish from a few pounds to about 20 pounds require a 7- to 10-weight rig, with greater reel capacity to spool the fly line and 100 yards of backing. A heavy outfit would consist of an 11- to 12-weight rod with 150 to 200 yards of backing on the reel, and a magnum-weight outfit for big game fish would require a 13-weight or heavier outfit, with an antireverse reel spooling the fly line plus 300 or more yards of backing. With heavy and magnum outfits, rod lifting power and strength are as important as casting ability.

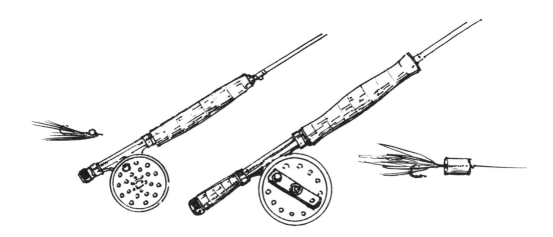

There are exceptions to the above, as when using a light 6- or 7-weight outfit for bonefish where 50 yards might be inadequate for their runs. A better rig would be a 6- or 7-weight with a reel holding 150 to 200 yards of backing. Most bonefish won't run anywhere near that far, but it's good insurance.

RODS
Blank Length
Since most saltwater fishing is in open-water situations, 9-foot rods are best. Rods longer than that are often whippy and difficult to cast. Shorter rods are better fish-fighting tools, but too short a rod can have less distance-casting ability.

Reel Seats
Reel seats should be anodized aluminum, long and sturdy enough to hold the foot of any saltwater fly reel. Avoid those with wood inserts. They should have two locknuts to hold the hood securely in place on the reel foot. Those with rubber O-rings between the two nuts prevent slippage. If lacking this, add an O-ring, available from any hardware store. Make sure that the reel seat is up-locking—the threads are located at the bottom of the rod—so as to provide a little extension and prevent clothing from catching in the reel.

Some reel seats have a permanent or detachable extension butt to allow greater leverage with the rod when propped against your body and to keep the reel spool from tangling with your clothing. The best extension butts measure 2 inches or less; longer butts tend to tangle line.

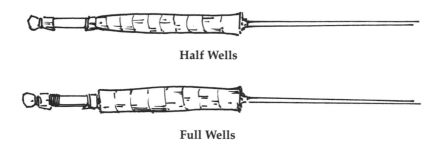

Half Wells

Full Wells

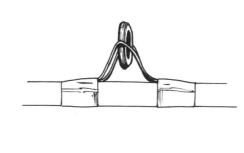

Full Wells with fighting grip

Grips

Grips should be cork half-Wells or full-Wells shape. If half-Wells, make sure that it is not put on backward. The swollen part of the grip must be at the front end to aid in punching out a cast. Some big game rods have foam grips. This is fine, since they are used for sight fishing and cast infrequently. Many big game rods also have a fighting grip—a short, slim grip just forward of the casting grip to aid in lifting and turning fish.

Guides

The best guides are chromed stainless steel snake guides or large, single-foot ceramics. Several stripping guides, almost like large spinning guides to aid line flow, are a must on the butt end. On any rod size 8 and above, size 6 snake guides (the largest) or size 12 ceramics should be used. Up to three stripping guides are best, the largest at least a size 12 on small rods, size 16 on rods to 9-weight, and size 20 to 25 on larger rods.

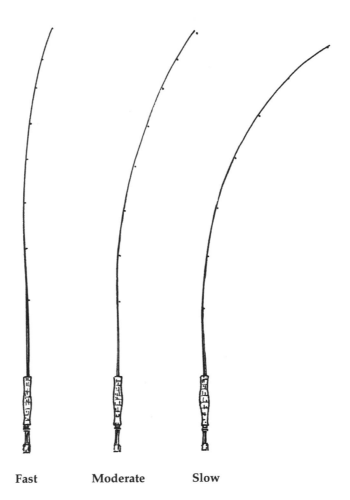

Fast   Moderate   Slow

Action
Action refers to how the rod bends—fast, with just the tip end bending markedly; moderate, bending well down in the rod; or slow, bending down into the grip area. For salt water, choose moderate to moderate-fast, since this gives you good casting range and the ability to throw tight loops, along with plenty of power (strength) in the butt to fight and land fish.

Power
The power of a rod is the resistance to bending. It affects casting and fighting fish. It translates into the line weight that can be used, since the line is the weight cast by the rod. The fly just goes along for the ride. Power sufficient for the chosen line, indicated on the rod, and the proper action result in a good rod.

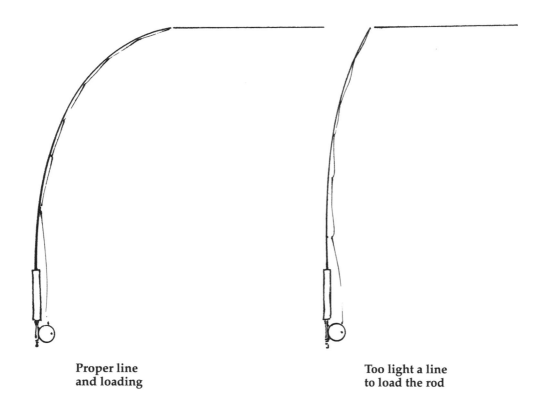

**Proper line
and loading**

**Too light a line
to load the rod**

Weight, or Line Size

Rods are sized by the weight of line that can be easily cast, with this determined by the weight in grains of the first 30 feet of line, although currently the American Fly Fishing Trade Association (AFFTA) is considering some changes. Casting too heavy a line, or using too light a rod, will require slowed timing or may strain tackle. Too light a line or too heavy a rod will make casting difficult. Fly lines and rods have a number system, in which typical rods and lines for salt water range from size 6 through 12, with lighter and heavier available.

REELS

Construction

Saltwater fly reels must resist corrosion, and anodized aluminum is the material of choice. They may be of machined bar stock, which is expensive, or cast aluminum. Some reels are made of corrosion-proof graphite. The springs, cogs, pawls, drags, handles, feet, and other parts are often of stainless steel but should be checked and cleaned frequently.

Size

Line capacity, both backing and fly line, is more important in saltwater than in freshwater fly fishing, since ocean fish are stronger than freshwater fish. Most manufacturers provide charts that show the line capacity in 20-pound (sometimes 30-pound) Dacron backing, with various fly lines for each reel.

Size is also important in retrieving line, since most reels are single-action—one turn of the handle makes one turn of the spool. The larger the reel spool diameter, the more line retrieved with each handle turn.

Right- or Left-Hand Drive

Reels are made to be retrieved right-handed or left-handed. Right-handed means retrieving line (turning the spool handle) with the right hand while holding the rod with the left. Left-handed is reversed. If you are a right-handed caster with a right-hand reel, you must switch hands after striking a fish to hold the rod with your left hand and retrieve with your right. Most anglers use this method, and experts suggest reeling with your dominant hand.

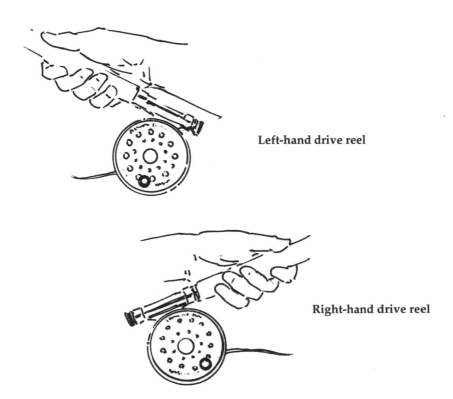

Left-hand drive reel

Right-hand drive reel

To change a reel, should you decide to switch, you must remove all the line and backing, reverse the drag plate or pawls, then rewind all the line. This is easy to do on some reels, requires tools on others, and cannot be changed on some factory-set reels. Cassette reels have a cassette that can be removed and switched on the spool.

Drag

All fly reels require a drag, but the stronger saltwater fish require a better drag than needed in fresh water. Drags work like car brakes, using cork and synthetic surfaces and drum, caliper, and disk systems to control resistance to spool rotation. Controls allow more or less drag as required by your fishing situation, the type of fish you're after, and the strength of your tippet. A drag must be smooth, with no or little inertial resistance when a fish begins a run.

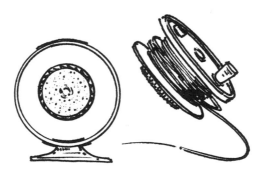

Action or Types

Within reason, any reel can be used for any fish, provided that it has a good drag and sufficient line capacity. Several types are available, including direct-drive, antireverse, multiplier, and large arbor reels. The choice of reel type is somewhat subjective, provided that you have the basics of line capacity and durability. Some anglers like antireverse reels for all their fishing; others like direct-drive even for big game fishing.

  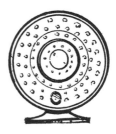

Direct-drive   **Antireverse**   **Large arbor**

Direct-Drive. Direct-drive reels have a handle attached to the spool so that one turn of the handle results in one turn of the spool. The advantage is direct control of the reel spool. The disadvantage is that as a fish runs, the handle turns and can become a knuckle buster.

Antireverse. Antireverse reels have a handle on a separate plate or bar rather than the reel spool. Turning the handle turns the spool, but only until line resistance is met, at which point you can turn the handle against the drag but will not turn the spool. The big advantage is safety, because the handle will not turn when a fish takes line. These reels are ideal for larger fish, where the drag is set heavier and there is more likelihood of long runs.

Multiplier. Multiplier reels have the handle separated from the spool and have additional gearing that allows you to make more than one turn of the spool with each turn of the handle. Typical reels have about a 1.5:1 or 2:1 gear ratio. Of the few made, most are not specifically designed for salt water.

Large Arbor. Large arbor reels are a new trend. The larger spool size and arbor results in a larger-diameter reel, which has the same line capacity as a smaller-diameter reel but has the ability to retrieve line faster.

Dual Mode. A few new reels have internal mechanisms that make them direct-drive when you turn the handle but antireverse when the handle is released, which means that the handle will not turn on a run. They would seem to provide the best of both worlds.

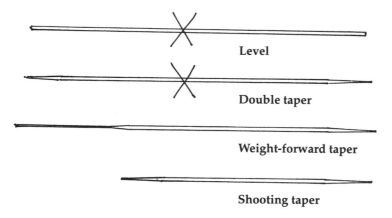

Level

Double taper

Weight-forward taper

Shooting taper

LINES

Types

Fly lines come in a number of basic types: level, double taper, weight-forward taper, and shooting taper, or shooting head. The only lines for salt water are the weight-forward taper and the shooting taper. Level line does not cast well, and double-taper lines are not designed for distance. Weight-forward tapers come in a number of subcategories, with special tapers for billfish, bonefish, stripers, tarpon, windy conditions, hot weather, and cold water. These vary by construction (for hot or cold climates), the length of the belly, the weight of the line, and the taper on the front end to turn over flies.

Weights

Lines vary by weight, based on the first 30 feet. Considering the range of saltwater fly fishing for everything from ½-pound white perch to 100-pound-plus billfish, suitable line weights can vary from size 6 through size 15 or even larger. Pick a fly line capable of casting and turning over the fly necessary to attract the fish sought, and match it to a rod capable of handling and landing the fish. You can effectively fish with too heavy an outfit, but you can't handle the fish or throw the fly easily if the line or rod is too light.

Many anglers today are fishing lines measured in grains rather than line size and are severely overlining their rods. The following are the grain weight standards used by the major line companies and their equivalent line weights.

In size 7 and larger, line weight standards are now changing from those set in 1961. The first 40 feet of line are now weighed, rather than the first 30 feet.

Standard spey lines, not applicable to salt water, will be slightly different and are not listed here. Short-head weight-forward (55 feet or less) and shooting-taper spey lines are included. The old and proposed standards are as follows:

LINE WEIGHT STANDARDS

Line Weight	Old Weight grains	Proposed New Weight grains/grams	Spey Line grains/grams
	(30-ft. weight) (pre-1999 Lines)	(40-ft. weight) (1999 Lines)	Shooting tapers or weight forwards with 55-foot-or-less heads measured at 55 feet
1 (not standard)	60	—	—
2	80	—	—
3	100	—	—
4	120	—	—
5	140	—	—
6	160	—	300/19.4
7	185	234/15.14	375/24.3
8	210	286/18.56	450/29.2
9	240	327/21.17	550/35.6
10	280	384/24.87	650/42.1
11	330	387/25.06	750/48.6
12	380	443/28.71	850/55.1

(larger sizes below are nonstandard in pre-1999 lines, but weights approximating these are used by most manufacturers)

13	430	517/33.47	950/61.6
14	480	583/37.78	—
15	530	626/40.56	—
16	580	—	—
17	630	—	—
18	680	—	—
19	730	—	—
20	780	—	—
21	830	—	—

At this writing, pre-1999 lines above size 12 are not standard, but manufacturers agree that each line above size 12 shall increase by 50 grains. Lines of up to 850 grains (Scientific Anglers), 750 grains (Teeny), and 625 grains (Cortland)—approximately sizes 21½, 19½, and 17—are also available.

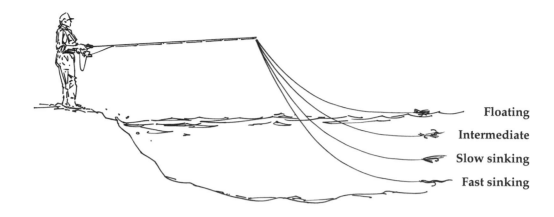

Sink Rate

In addition to different tapers, lines are made to float or to sink at various sink rates. Manufacturers list the sink rate in inches per second. A typical reading would be 7–9 ips, meaning 7 to 9 inches per second. This allows fishing at a controlled depth or sinking a fly rapidly to get to fish. Lines with a sinking-tip section and floating rear section allow you to fish specific depths and to more easily pick line up off the water. Sinking and sinking-tip lines are also available with proposed new (1999) industry-standard sink rates. Manufacturers are now using industry-standard numbers 1 through 10 to indicate the approximate sink rate in inches per second, plus or minus ½ inch. These proposed new standardized sink rates are as follows:

Sink Rate Number	Sink Rate
1	½"–1½"
2	1½"–2½"
3	2½"–3½"
4	3½"–4½"
5	4½"–5½"
6	5½"–6½"
7	6½"–7½"
8	7½"–8½"
9	8½"–9½"
10	9½"–10½"

	Backing		Weight-forward line		Leader

	Backing		Running line		Shooting taper		Leader

Kinds of Lines

Weight-Forward Lines. Weight-forward lines, in which the heaviest part of the line is in the forward section, are the best for most saltwater fly fishing. They allow you to cast long distances and to cast and shoot line with the minimum number of false casts.

Shooting Tapers. Shooting tapers are specialized lines, usually about 30 to 40 feet long. They allow greater casting distance than weight-forward lines but require practice to use well. They are primarily designed for false casting the shooting taper, and then, with a powerful forward cast, releasing the line to make a long cast as the heavy shooting taper carries a thin shooting line. Double-taper lines can be cut down to make two or more 30- to 37-foot-long shooting tapers.

Running or Shooting Line. Running line, usually 100 feet, is attached to the back of the short shooting taper. Since the shooting tapers are false-cast with the head out of the guides and the line released on a final forward cast, the running line in effect becomes part of the fly line and is shot to the target. When added to the shooting taper, usually about 30 to 37 feet, this makes a fishable line of up to 137 feet. Thin-diameter level lines can be used as shooting lines with shooting tapers.

Backing

Many saltwater fish will run farther than the length of a fly line—80 to 105 feet—or a shooting taper setup as described above. Thus backing is necessary in all saltwater fly fishing. Braided Dacron line or gel-spun polyethylene lines may be used for backing. Both have little stretch; Dacron has about 6 to 7 percent stretch, and gel-spun lines about 2 to 3 percent. Both pack on the reel well when spooling and fighting fish and do not expand to cause reel spool problems.

Typical backing is 20- or 30-pound-test Dacron. The 20-pound-test is fine for outfits to about 8-weight. The 30-pound-test is better for big fish, tough fights, long use, and for any outfit 9-weight and heavier. Some anglers for tuna or other big fish such as sharks, which might abrade the line with their bodies during the fight, use 50-pound-test Dacron backing or 80-pound-test gel-spun, which has the diameter of about 20-pound-test Dacron. Though thinner, the gel-spun lines have abrasion resistance equal to or slightly higher than larger-diameter Dacron lines. The advantage of the gel-spun lines is that because they are thinner for the test strength, you can have greater line capacity on a reel or use a heavier pound-test backing. With the thin diameter of the gel-spun lines, it must be packed on tight to prevent it from digging into coils of the backing. Also use care to avoid finger cuts while playing fish.

The amount of backing that can be spooled onto a reel is relative to the diameter, as shown in the accompanying tables for Dacron backing.

DACRON LINE CAPACITY CONVERSIONS IN YARDS

Line Test	Capacity		
20	100 yards	145 yards	240 yards
30	70 yards	100 yards	165 yards
50	40 yards	60 yards	100 yards

DACRON LINE CAPACITY CONVERSIONS IN PERCENT

Line Test	Percent Adjustments		
20	Base	45% more	140% more
30	30% less	Base	65% more
50	60% less	40% less	Base

Line Color
Lines are available in the full spectrum of colors. Most floating lines are light colored; most sinking lines are dark colored (tips only on sinking-tip lines). If fishing shallows, choose light-colored lines that will match the bottom color and are less likely to spook fish on a cast. Clear lines—mostly slow sinking and made by all manufacturers—are almost invisible in the air and are ideal for shallow-water flats fishing.

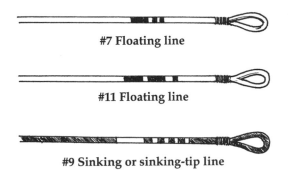

#7 Floating line

#11 Floating line

#9 Sinking or sinking-tip line

Marking Fly Lines

To avoid ending up with unidentified lines, Lefty Kreh developed a system of marking lines using colored bands. A broad band indicates the number 5, a narrow band indicates 1, and so on. You can use a black permanent felt-tip pen on light-colored line and a white opaque marker or typewriter correction fluid covered with clear flexible sealer on dark or sinking-tip lines. I've also started marking (about 1 foot up from the above size markings) fly lines with the sink rate, as per the new AFFTA standards.

LEADERS

Length

Leader length varies with the type of line used. Use a long leader—9 to 10 feet—for fishing floating or slow-sinking lines or in clear-water flats situations. For breaking fish, use an 8-foot leader. For fishing clear water or for spooky fish, use a 10- to 15-foot leader. Use a short leader of no more than 3 to 4 feet when fishing sinking or sinking-tip lines. This prevents the fly from being suspended higher in the water column than the line. An exception is when fishing around rocks or coral, where a long, tough leader is necessary to avoid cutting or abrading expensive fly line.

Shorten or lengthen leaders as required. Leaders must be long enough to keep the fish from being spooked by the fly line and provide a strong connection to allow landing the fish.

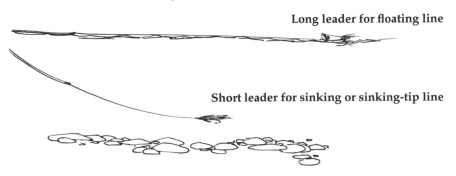

Long leader for floating line

Short leader for sinking or sinking-tip line

Taper

Most leaders are tapered from a heavy butt section to a thin section—called a tippet—tied to the fly. Exceptions are very short level leaders used with sinking lines and some big game leaders where the emphasis is on strength. Typical tapers include a butt section of 30- to 50-pound-test mono tied with blood knots to sections of successively lighter mono and ending with a thin tippet that might range from 4-pound-test for some bonefish to 20-pound-test or more for big fish. Commercially available knotless leaders often have too-thin butt sections. Tie a commercial leader to a heavy butt end of mono already attached to your fly line.

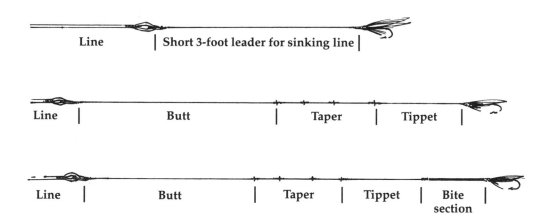

Line | Short 3-foot leader for sinking line |

Line | Butt | Taper | Tippet |

Line | Butt | Taper | Tippet | Bite section |

Tippet

Tippets are typically monofilament, clear or mist colored to match water color. Consider fluorocarbon tippets in very clear water and with spooky fish, since the refractive index is much closer to water than that of mono, making them less visible. Tippets are 18 to 24 inches long.

A good rule of thumb for tippet strength is to start with a tippet in pound strength approximately the line weight of the rod. Thus for a 6-weight rod, use a 6-pound-test tippet; for a 9-weight rod, use an 8- or 10-pound-test tippet; and for a 14-weight rod, use a 12- or 15-pound-test tippet. Lighter tippets can be used but have an increased risk of breakage. Use heavier tippets if fishing around structure or weeds.

Bite Leaders or Sections

Toothy fish, such as bluefish, barracuda, mackerel, and sharks, will bite through mono tippets. Bite leader sections of heavy mono, single-strand wire, or braided wire, usually about a foot long, will prevent this. Heavy mono will work on some fish, but wire is always better, unless the fish is leader shy. Typical bite sections are tied to the tippet at one end, if a tippet is used, and the fly at the other. Special connections are required to attach wire to the fly and the tippet or leader.

Leader Formulas

There are some standard formulas to make leaders. One recommends a butt section of 40 percent of the length, the tapered portion 40 percent of the total length, and the tippet 20 percent. A bite section, if used, is added to this. Another formula suggests 60 percent for the butt section, 20 percent for the midsection, and 20 percent for the tippet. This is better for large bugs and bulky flies that otherwise would be difficult to turn over.

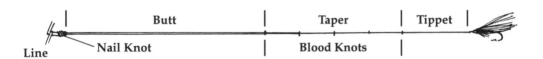

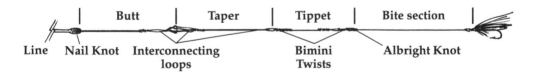

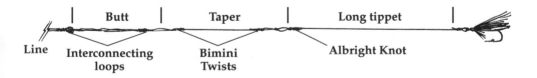

Storage
Both commercial and homemade leaders are best stored in coils. Spools can be strung together in sequence on a string. When boat fishing, you can use a leader box specifically designed for this. These hold several spools.

KNOTS
To join sections of your fly-line system, you can use a series of knots, as detailed below, or loop-to-loop connections.

Learn and practice knots at home before going out on the water. Make knots exactly as described. Use saliva as a lubricant when pulling up knots to prevent weakening heat and friction. Test all knots after tying. If a knot does not look right, cut and retie. Coat all knots with glue to prevent slippage and strengthen the knot. You can use a cyanoacrylate glue, or superglue, on most fishing knots. Fishin' Glue is one such glue that works on wet line. Flexible sealers such as Pliobond and UltraFlex are good for protecting loop knots and other bulky line knots. UltraFlex is a little thick but can be thinned, and its working life extended, by using methyl ethyl ketone (MEK) thinner, available at hardware stores. You can also use a solvent-based nail polish remover, but you should test first with a small amount of glue, as brands differ.

Backing to Reel

Attach backing to the reel by looping the backing around the reel arbor, knot around the standing line with an overhand knot, and finish with an overhand knot in the tag end to prevent slippage. If the loop slips on the arbor, secure it with a small piece of tape.

Arbor Knot

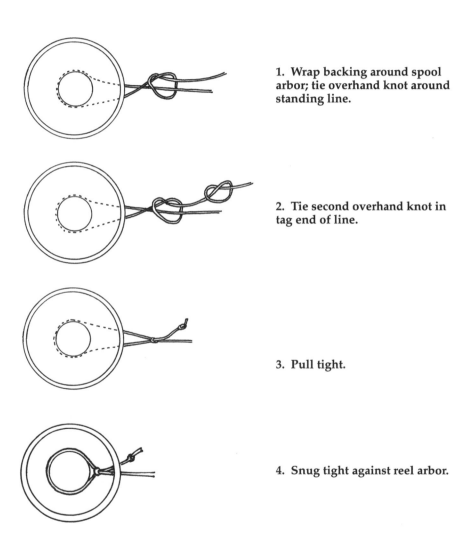

1. **Wrap backing around spool arbor; tie overhand knot around standing line.**

2. **Tie second overhand knot in tag end of line.**

3. **Pull tight.**

4. **Snug tight against reel arbor.**

Backing to Line

One way to attach the backing to the fly line is with an Albright knot. Here you double the fly line and wrap the backing around it, then tuck it into the loop to finish or nail-knot the backing to the fly line. If using a nail knot, pull it up slowly to prevent tangles.

Albright Knot

1. **Run backing line through or parallel to loop made in end of fly line.**

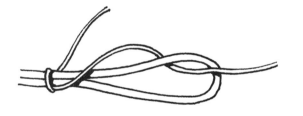

2. **Wrap backing around standing line and doubled fly line.**

3. **After 12 to 15 turns around the loop, tuck the tag end through the loop.**

4. **Slide the wraps forward to secure the tag end and pull tight.**

Line to Leader

Nail knots or needle knots are best to permanently connect the leader butt to the fly line. A needle knot is a variation of the nail knot in which the butt end of the leader is threaded through the center core of the fly line, through the side, and then nail-knotted to the line.

Nail Knot

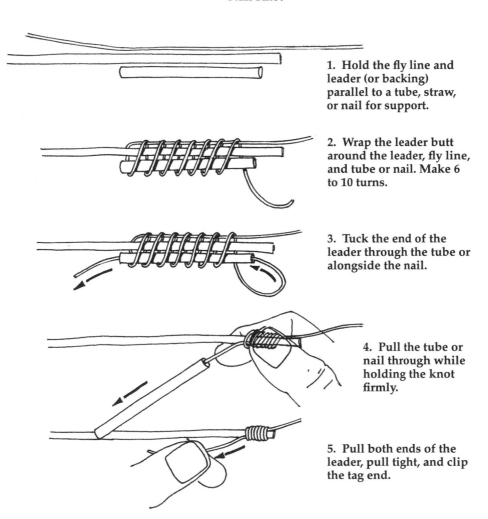

1. Hold the fly line and leader (or backing) parallel to a tube, straw, or nail for support.

2. Wrap the leader butt around the leader, fly line, and tube or nail. Make 6 to 10 turns.

3. Tuck the end of the leader through the tube or alongside the nail.

4. Pull the tube or nail through while holding the knot firmly.

5. Pull both ends of the leader, pull tight, and clip the tag end.

Leader Knots

Attach sections of mono together to make or modify a leader with a blood knot.

Blood Knot

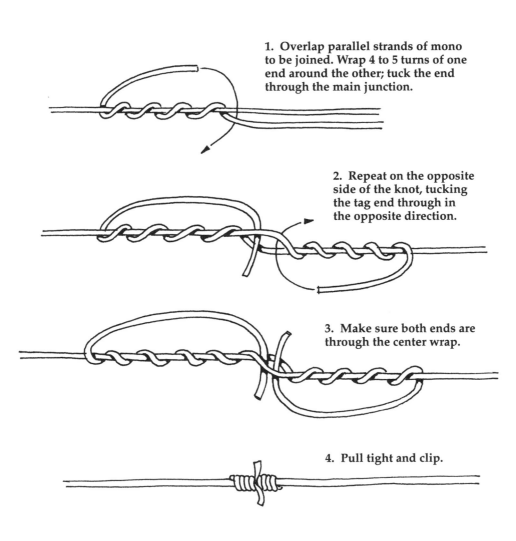

1. **Overlap parallel strands of mono to be joined. Wrap 4 to 5 turns of one end around the other; tuck the end through the main junction.**

2. **Repeat on the opposite side of the knot, tucking the tag end through in the opposite direction.**

3. **Make sure both ends are through the center wrap.**

4. **Pull tight and clip.**

Dropper Connections

In some fishing, you might want to add a second fly. Do this by making an in-line dropper loop in the leader or a long tippet section. Another way to do this is to make the dropper loop and clip one end to make a dropper section to which a second fly can be tied. Do not add a dropper if fishing for toothy fish; a hit on the dropper may cut the main leader as the dropper fly lies against it on the retrieve.

In-Line Dropper Loop

2. Make 3 to 4 turns of doubled leader.

1. Form loop in leader.

3. Pull loop through center of wraps formed.

4. Pull up carefully.

5. Pull tight. Dropper may be attached using interconnecting loops or one end cut to form dropper tippet.

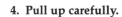

Tippet to Bite Leader

If using heavy mono or braided wire for a bite section, tie it to the tippet using an Albright knot, folding over the heavy mono or wire and wrapping with the light section. For maximum strength in the tippet, tie a Bimini loop and use the doubled line of the loop to tie the Albright to the bite leader. Another possibility with mono is to use a reverse of the Albright knot in which the heavy mono is wrapped (three times only) around the double strands of a loop knot like a small Bimini. If using single-strand wire, make a haywire twist in the wire, and then tie the leader or tippet to it with an improved clinch knot.

Reverse Albright Knot

1. Run heavy mono through or parallel to the loop made in lighter mono.

2. Begin to wrap heavy mono around the lighter-line loop.

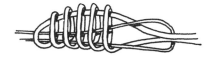

3. Make 3 to 5 wraps of the heavy mono around the light mono loop.

4. Slowly pull the knot tight.

5. Snug the knot to secure and clip end.

Leader to Fly

Tie light mono or fluorocarbon tippets to the fly using an improved clinch knot or Palomar knot. With a heavy mono bite tippet, use an improved clinch knot with only three turns around the standing line. For a loose connection to get maximum movement from a fly, use a Homer Rhode loop knot. Use *only* with heavy mono, since this does not have high knot strength. For single-strand wire, use a haywire twist on the fly. For braided wire, use a figure-eight knot or attach with a loop using a crimped leader sleeve.

Improved Clinch Knot

1. Run leader through hook eye, wrap around standing part of the leader 5 turns, and tuck through open loop then back through loop just formed.

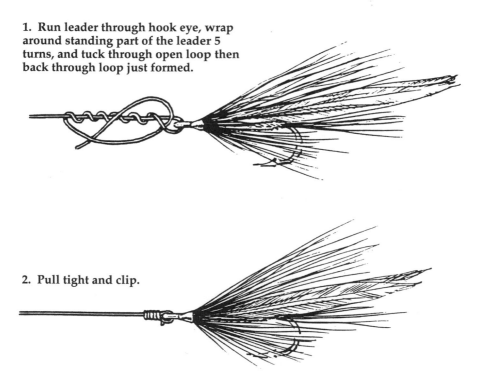

2. Pull tight and clip.

Palomar Knot

1. Double the leader tippet; run through eye of fly.

2. Make overhand knot in the doubled leader tippet.

3. Run loop formed over and around fly.

4. Pull tight and clip.

Homer Rhode Knot

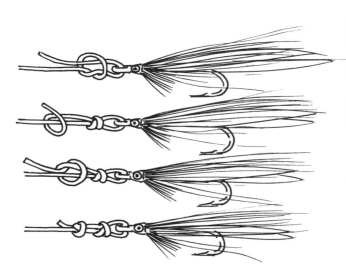

1. Make overhand knot in shock tippet, then run end through fly hook eye and back through the overhand knot.

2. Wrap tag end of leader around the line to begin making second overhand knot.

3. Complete overhand knot around leader.

4. Pull tight; pull on leader to snug knots and make larger loop.

Haywire Twist

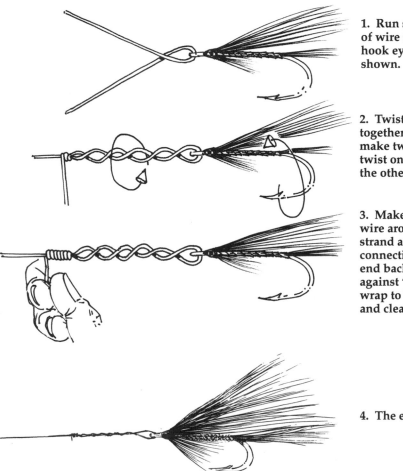

1. Run single strand of wire through fly hook eye and cross as shown.

2. Twist two wires together loosely to make twist; do *not* twist one wire around the other.

3. Make tight wrap of wire around main strand at end to secure connection; work tag end back and forth against "shoulder" of wrap to break close and cleanly.

4. The end result.

Figure-Eight Knot for Braided Wire

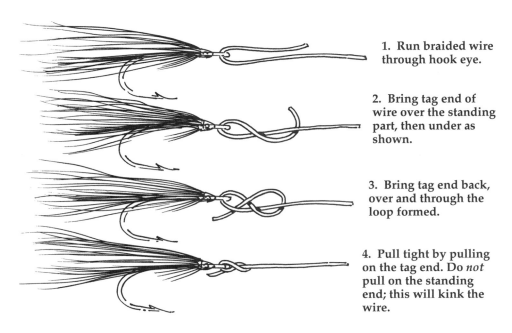

1. Run braided wire through hook eye.

2. Bring tag end of wire over the standing part, then under as shown.

3. Bring tag end back, over and through the loop formed.

4. Pull tight by pulling on the tag end. Do *not* pull on the standing end; this will kink the wire.

Crimped Leader Sleeve Loop

1. Run mono or braided wire through leader sleeve, then through hook eye.

2. Continue running tag end of mono or wire back through the leader sleeve.

3. Make tag end flush or just barely extending from leader sleeve and crimp tight with crimping pliers.

4. Completed crimp and loop.

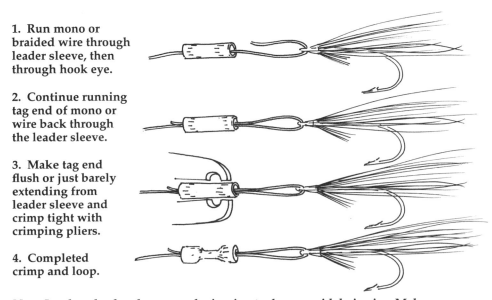

Note: Leaders, leader sleeves, and crimping tools vary widely in size. Make sure they all match for a proper, strong connection.

Loop-to-Loop Connections

An excellent alternative to the above knots is loop-to-loop connections to join sections of the fly-line system. Premade braided loops can be slipped over, and fastened to, the fly line. Another alternative is to fold the end of the fly line over itself, wrap with fly-tying thread (whip-finish), and seal with flexible cement such as Pliobond or UltraFlex. Make loops in the backing using a needle splice in hollow line or by tying a Bimini. Make mono loops using a surgeon's loop knot, perfection loop knot, or figure-eight loop knot, all of which lie straight. Use these loops to connect backing, line, leader, tippet, and bite sections.

Attaching Braided Leader Loop

1. Choose correct size of braided loop for the line used. (Sizes vary.)

2. Work braided loop onto the end of the fly line (works like a Chinese finger puzzle).

3. Secure at both ends with nail knots or whipped fly-tying thread; coat with flexible sealer for protection.

Making a whipped loop in end of fly line

1. Fold end of fly line over itself.

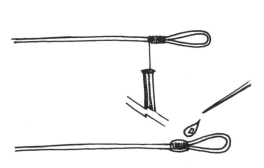

2. Wrap with fly-tying thread (hold both sides of wrap and swing bobbin around the line to wrap). Secure with whip finish.

3. Seal with flexible sealer to protect.

Bimini Twist

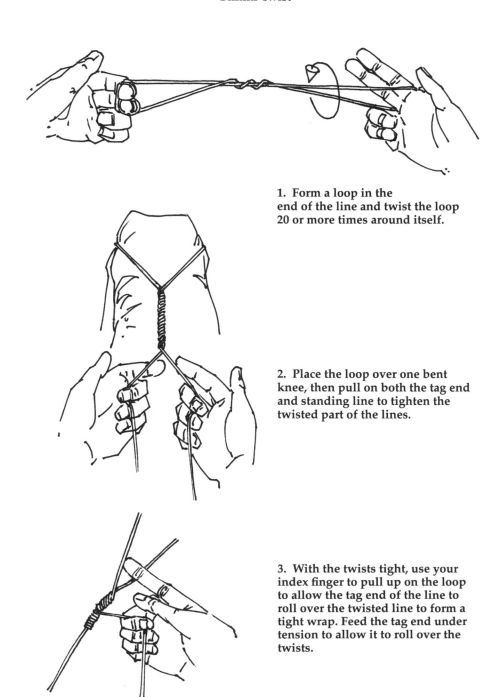

1. Form a loop in the
end of the line and twist the loop
20 or more times around itself.

2. Place the loop over one bent
knee, then pull on both the tag end
and standing line to tighten the
twisted part of the lines.

3. With the twists tight, use your
index finger to pull up on the loop
to allow the tag end of the line to
roll over the twisted line to form a
tight wrap. Feed the tag end under
tension to allow it to roll over the
twists.

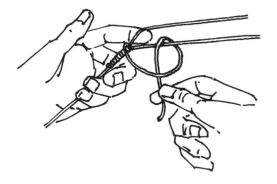

4. At the bottom of the twist with the wrapped line over it, use the tag end to make a half hitch around one leg of the formed loop.

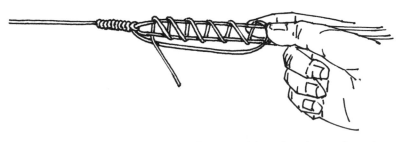

5. Make a second half hitch around the second leg, then form a large loop with the tag end of the line and make up to 6 wraps around the two legs of the loop (held parallel to each other), working back toward the knot. Tuck the tag end between the newly formed loop and the wrap around the two legs of the Bimini.

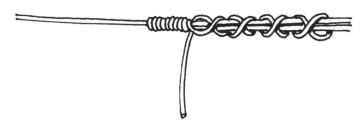

6. Slowly, with saliva lubrication, pull up on the tag end to secure the locking wrap. Pull back on the locking twists as you do this to avoid tangles.

7. Completed, locked Bimini.

Surgeon's Loop Knot

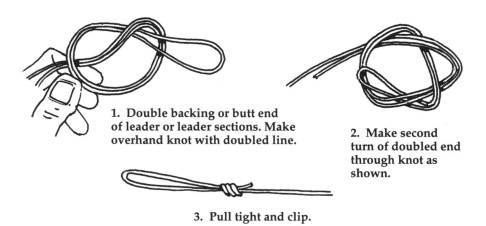

1. Double backing or butt end of leader or leader sections. Make overhand knot with doubled line.

2. Make second turn of doubled end through knot as shown.

3. Pull tight and clip.

Figure-Eight Loop Knot

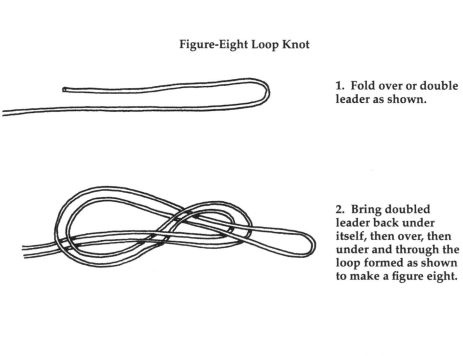

1. Fold over or double leader as shown.

2. Bring doubled leader back under itself, then over, then under and through the loop formed as shown to make a figure eight.

3. Pull tight and clip excess leader.

Perfection Loop Knot

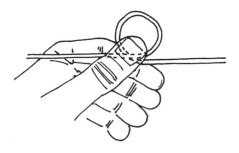

1. Hold line with index finger and thumb and fold over the line to form a loop as shown, with the tag end of the loop under the standing line. (Each step of this tying process is completed with the thumb and index finger holding these loops, but the fingers are not shown in subsequent illustrations for clarity.)

2. Form another small loop over the top of the first loop and over the thumb holding the original loop. Bring the tag end around and under the first loop.

3. Bring the tag end once again over and across the loops and between the two loops already formed.

4. Holding the tag end in place between the two loops, bring the top loop down through the original (bottom) loop.

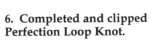

5. Hold the standing part, tag end, and final formed loop and pull all three gently to lock the loop knot in place.

6. Completed and clipped Perfection Loop Knot.

Interconnecting loops should lock together as in 1, not form a girth hitch as in 2.

Lead-Core Leader Sections

Loop-to-loop connections allow insertion of short lengths (usually 1 to several feet) of lead-core line, looped at both ends, to aid in sinking a fly. Use these between the end of the line and the leader butt, in the center of the leader, or between the leader and tippet. They are commercially available or readily made from lengths of lead-core line, cut to length and with a loop knot on each end. Seal the knot with Pliobond or UltraFlex. Lead-core line varies from 18- to 45-pound-test—use line of sufficient strength.

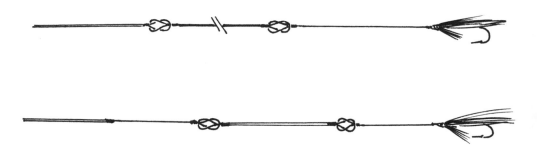

Interconnecting loops make it easy to add short lengths of lead-core sinking sections in the middle of a leader or between the line and leader.

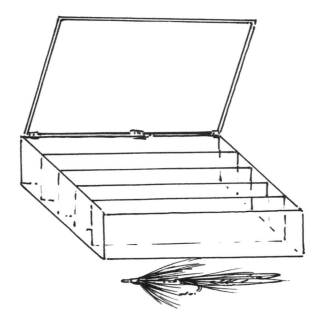

FLY CONTAINERS

Fly boxes with large compartments are necessary for the larger flies used. The best boxes for long flies, such as streamers, have compartments running lengthwise. Smaller flies can be stored in standard compartment boxes. Fly boxes with clips are good but can dull hooks. Check and sharpen hooks from such boxes before each use. Soft containers, such as the clear-pocket tackle bags designed for lures, also work well.

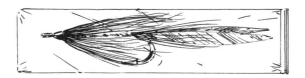

Avoid fly boxes containing any foam, since they do not hold flies well, quickly become punctured, and allow fly hooks to rust. Avoid lamb's wool or leather fly wallets for the same reason. An ideal system for large streamer flies is to use 1½-by-9-inch plastic envelopes to store one or two flies each, and placed in a suitable box.

ESSENTIAL ACCESSORIES

Clippers. You'll need clippers to cut mono. Fisherman's clippers or fingernail clippers both work fine.

Hook Hone. A hook hone or file is an essential tool for serious fly fishing, since dull hooks lose fish or won't hook them. The best file for small flies is a diamond dust file. A small hardware file is ideal for larger flies, but store it in a sheath soaked with WD-40 to prevent rust.

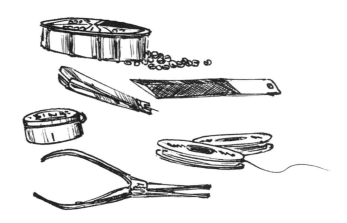

Hemostats. Hemostats make it easy to remove flies from fish. Get those with a long nose for easy catch-and-release fishing and safely handling toothy fish.

Pliers. Pliers are useful for holding large flies while sharpening them, removing flies from fish, tightening nuts on gear in an emergency, and other tasks.

Leader and Fly Sink. Use leader or fly sink when fishing sinking flies. An alternative is to wet a fly with mud or sand.

Sunglasses. Polarizing sunglasses are a must. Even if you're not sight fishing, they'll help you spot underwater structure or find rip lines and oil slicks. Prescription polarizing glasses are available, even in bifocal styles to aid in tying knots. Glasses with side shields will help eliminate glare. Colors of glasses vary. Gray or brown is best for high-contrast, sunny conditions; yellow works well for low-light, low-contrast conditions. All polarizers work best with the sun at your back or side, and turning your head from side to side sometimes helps you see through water.

Cap. A cap works in concert with your sunglasses to prevent overhead glare. The cap should have a dark underbrim. Some caps have rear flaps or brims to protect the neck.

Sunscreen. Much saltwater fly fishing is done in the summer or in tropical areas. Always use sunscreens with an SPF of at least 15. Coat all exposed areas liberally and reapply frequently.

Nets. Nets are great fish-landing devices, although they are more widely used in fresh water than salt. Boat nets should have a long handle and large frame; wading nets should have a short handle and easy-release snap to remove from the back of a fishing vest.

Catch-and-release nets should have a woven, rubber-coated, or, best, rubber mesh to prevent harm to the fish and its protective slime coating. Avoid nets that have bright mesh—fish will see it and spook—or floating polypropylene netting, which fish will feel and spook.

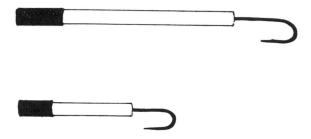

Gaffs. Long-handled landing gaffs and short-handled release gaffs are both used in saltwater fly fishing. Use a long-handled gaff to body-gaff a fish that you wish to keep. Use a short-handled gaff to gaff a fish up through the lower lip to stabilize it so that you can remove the fly and release the fish. Gaffs for most fishing should have a 3- to 4-inch gap and a 3- to 5-foot-long handle for boat fishing or a 1-foot-long handle for lipping and release fishing.

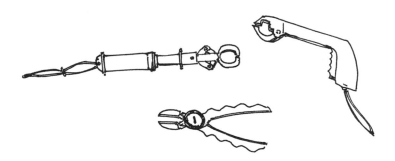

Lippers. Lippers look like large-jawed pliers and are used to lip-land fish. Catch-and-release styles have jaws that meet only on the ends to prevent damaging the fish. Some lippers also weigh your catch.

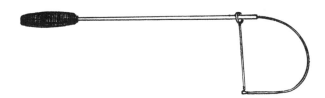

Tailers. Tailers are used more in freshwater salmon fishing but are also good for salt water, particularly to land and control toothy fish such as sharks.

J-shaped de-hooker

Q-shaped de-hooker

Ketchum Release

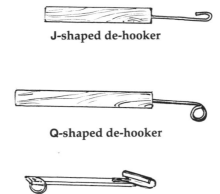

Dehookers. Dehookers vary widely. The end can look like a J, an overlapping loop, or Q. To use, grab the fly by the bend of the hook with the J-shaped tool to pull the fly out, pulling up on the J tool and simultaneously down with the hook shank or leader. For deeply hooked fish, the Q-shaped tool allows you to run the tool over the line and around the bend of the fly to push down on the fly and back it out of the fish.

Another excellent tool is the sleevelike Ketchum Release, available in two handle lengths and three sizes for saltwater fishing. Use the long handle length for boat fishing or toothy fish.

Stripping Baskets. When wading, line in the water makes casting difficult. Surface tension prevents shooting the line. Stripping baskets or line tenders prevent these problems. They are also useful in boats to prevent line from tangling with other tackle. The best baskets have holes in the bottom to release water—a must for wading—and nubs in the bottom to hold the line from blowing around. Baskets should fit low on the thigh of your line-hand leg, since stripping is a sideways move. Lacking a suitable commercial stripping basket, you can make your own from a belt or bungee cord and a small, open-weave laundry basket.

OPTIONAL ACCESSORIES

Flashlight. A flashlight is a necessity for night fishing, and it's always a good idea to have one on hand. Get one that's tough and waterproof, and check the batteries frequently.

Thermometer. Saltwater fish react to temperature—tarpon must have 75 degrees, bonefish over 70 degrees. A thermometer can indicate water temperature to tell you when a previous cool night might have moved fish off a flat or excessive temperatures might have pushed fish deeper to cooler waters.

Knot Tier. Knot tiers are ideal for making simple knots and are recommended for those new to knot tying, for those who have poor eyesight, when tying knots at night, or in poor light.

Glasses Magnifier. Glasses magnifiers are similar to drugstore reading glasses but clip onto regular glasses or the brim of a cap and flip out of the way when not used. They are great for tying knots and threading tippets through the eye of the fly.

Fishing Gloves. Fishing gloves can be lightweight for summer sun protection or warm and heavier for cold-weather fishing. All styles leave one or more fingers free to tie flies and handle line. Some cold-weather styles have fold-over mitten-style tips to protect your hands when not tying knots. Gloves are also good to protect your fingers when a fish is running and taking backing.

WADING EQUIPMENT

Hip boots are two separate crotch-high boots held up with belt straps. Waders are chest-high and held up with suspenders. Both are available in self-contained boot-foot or stocking-foot styles and in many fabrics. The stocking waders or hip boots require wading shoes. All boots come in rubber-cleated, felt sole, and metal-cleated versions. Rubber soles are OK for general use or sandy bottoms, but use felt soles for rocky bottoms and metal cleats, often on felt soles, to cut through muck and algae when fishing from a rock jetty.

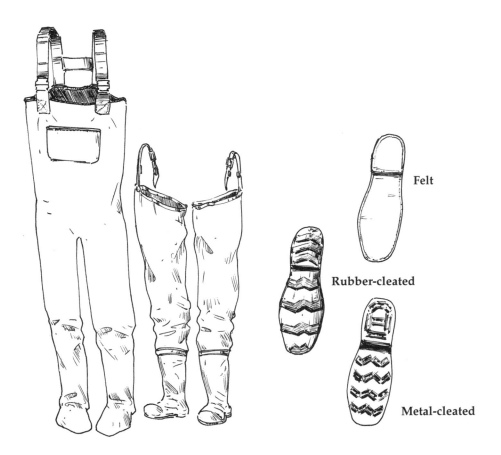

Felt

Rubber-cleated

Metal-cleated

Both waders and hip boots come in thin fabric for travel and thicker neoprene fabric. For all-around use, consider waders in a lightweight travel fabric and add long johns if wading in cold water.

Flats wading shoes are worn when wading wet. They are usually ankle-high, slip-over boots with a light sole to offer some protection against shells and sea urchins.

TACKLE CARE
Rods
A good way to clean rods is to take them into the shower with you and clean them with a sudsy brush or washcloth. Pay particular attention to guides, reel seats, and ferrules. Air-dry *completely* before storing in tubes. Do not store rods ferruled, since they can stick. If stuck, hold the two ends close to the ferrule and twist gently; do not hold or twist guides.

Reels
Wash reels in warm, sudsy water. If possible, remove the spool from the frame to soak for a few minutes. Use a small brush such as an old tooth-brush to gently scrub around crevices like the handle and reel foot to remove salt. Rinse thoroughly and dry. Do not spray with a demoistur-izer, since this may damage the fly line. Back off the drag after each fishing trip to keep it working smoothly.

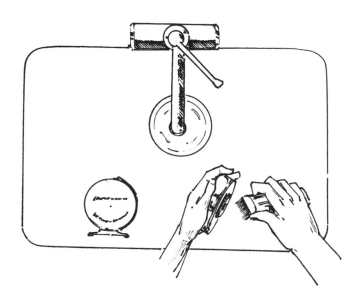

Lines

Make sure that lines are spooled correctly on the reel and that the reel is washed after each use. If the line is particularly dirty or salty, remove it from the reel onto a line-drying wheel, wash with warm fresh water, air-dry, and respool on the reel. This is also recommended for backing used in salt water. Most fly lines have a PVC coating that may be harmed by certain solvents and liquids such as gasoline, insect sprays, demoisturizers, or sunscreens. Wash your hands after using these or other products and before handling line. For floating line, add line dressing and then polish the line to remove any excess. Too much dressing left on the line will pick up dirt and damage the line.

Flies

Store flies in a proper fly box so that they are not compressed and the materials are not bent or folded. Since salt water is corrosive to hooks and other metallic materials used in flies, wash flies after use. Keep all flies used during fishing in a separate box or plastic bag, then wash these flies at home, dry thoroughly, and return to the fly box. If salt spray hits an open fly box or if a fly box falls into the water, wash the contents thoroughly in fresh water and air-dry completely.

Accessories

Any metallic fishing equipment, such as pliers, hemostats, or gaffs, should be washed in fresh water at the end of each fishing day. Tools with movable parts, such as pliers, should be washed, dried, and coated with a protective demoisturizing agent such as CRC or WD-40.

Clothing, Waders, Boots

Wash clothing and rinse waders or boots, dry, and then store properly. Store waders by folding and boxing carefully or hanging by the boot foot from racks made for this purpose.

Chapter 2

Flies

Flies are the lures fly fishermen use to catch fish. Fish hit flies for many reasons. Fish often mistake flies for food, especially those that simulate a natural food. Most flies are suggestive of baitfish or natural bait. Some fish attack flies by reflex even when not hungry. It is thought that shad and salmon do this when ascending rivers to spawn. It is not uncommon to catch a fish with a full stomach or the tail of a baitfish still sticking out of its throat. Interest by one fish in a fly may provoke a competitive reaction on the part of other fish. Some fish strike out of anger, because they do not want the fly, which appears to be a smaller sea-life form, in the area. This can be a territorial reflex.

FOODS

Saltwater fish eat a wide variety of foods, which can include fish, crustaceans, shellfish, and saltwater worms. The following are some common foods, any of which can be used as the basis for flies.

• **Baitfish.** Baitfish such as minnows, smelt, silversides, anchovies, sardines, mummichogs, shiners, killifish, pinfish, and even juvenile game fish are eaten by predators. These baitfish have different shapes. Typical ones include herring- or menhadenlike fish that have high, flat, thin bodies; slim, cigar-shaped fish such as anchovies and sand lance; and fat or stout fish such as mullet. To imitate a baitfish properly, the fly design and pattern must take into account the general shape, along with size and color.

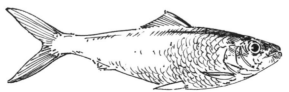

Alewife

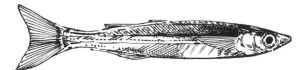

Shiner (spearing)

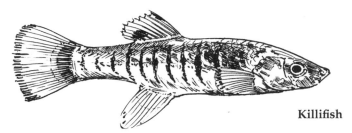

Killifish

Blue herring

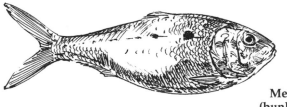

**Menhaden
(bunker, pogy)**

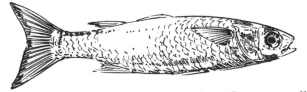

Common mullet

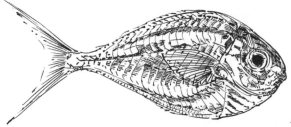

**Butterfish
(skipjack, sheepshead)**

• **Needlefish.** Needlefish are very slim and can be easily tied with long, sparse wings of synthetic materials.

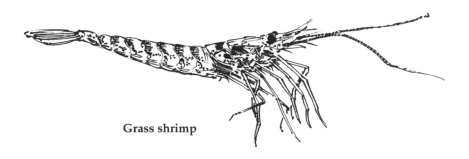

Grass shrimp

• **Shrimp.** Shrimp ties can be simple or complicated. In addition to the typical shrimp (we're all familiar with these) are mantis shrimp and snapping shrimp, which look more like small lobsters or crayfish.

Blue crab

• **Crabs.** Small crabs of all types are eaten by fish. These include blue crabs, green crabs, and mud crabs. Many patterns are available.

• **Lobster and spiny lobster.** Almost any freshwater crayfish pattern can be modified as a small lobster or saltwater crayfish. Fish eat these in small sizes.

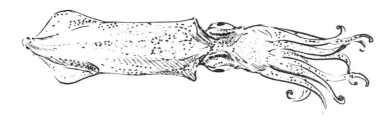

• **Squid.** Squid are eaten by most ocean fish. Many simple imitations are available.

• **Eels.** Eels are a popular inshore bait for striped bass and other coastal species. Any long, slim, black or dark olive fly works well.

Clam worm

• **Worms.** Certain saltwater worms are relished by game fish. Flies imitating worms are particularly good when the worms are spawning. Palolo worms are prevalent in southern waters, although predicting swarming and the resultant fish frenzy is difficult. Simple red streamer flies and similar patterns work well.

• **Sea urchins.** Tropical fish eat sea urchins, although there are few ties and only limited ways to fish these patterns.

• **Jellyfish.** Some predators feed on very small jellyfish, although there are few patterns available.

HOOKS
Hook Types
Saltwater patterns are tied on short-shank, regular-length-shank, and long-shank hooks. Best for general use are those with straight ringed eyes. Fly hooks should not be bent to one side, known as kirbed or offset. Long-shank hooks are used for streamers, lobster patterns, shrimp flies, and some baitfish imitations.

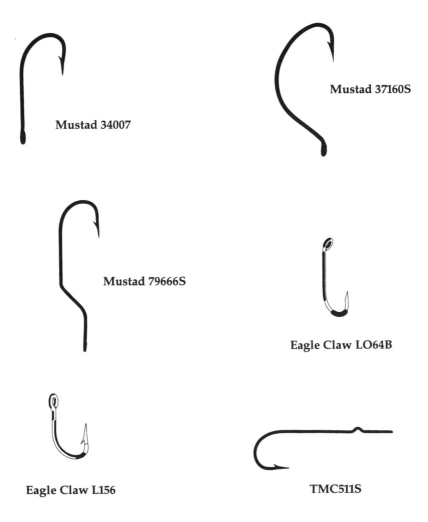

Mustad 34007

Mustad 37160S

Mustad 79666S

Eagle Claw LO64B

Eagle Claw L156

TMC511S

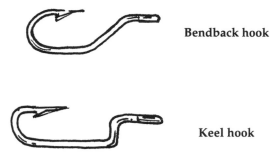

Bendback hook

Keel hook

Keel hooks and bendback hooks are specialty hooks made both to protect the hook point with the wing of the fly and to ride point-up. For better hooking, use pliers to slightly increase the hook gap.

Hook Materials
Hooks must be corrosion resistant. The best hooks are stainless steel or coated. Some anglers do not like stainless steel, arguing that it will not rust out of a fish's mouth should you break off a fish. Research shows, however, that fish will develop necrotic tissue, eventually creating a hole, around any hook, at which time it will fall out.

Sizes
Large sizes are dictated by the weight or bulk of the fly and your ability to cast it. You can go as small as you want, so long as you can hook and land with it. Typical sizes range from a size 8 for small fish such as perch, small bonefish, sea bass, or shad to sizes as large as 5/0 or 7/0 for big game fish such as sharks or billfish. Most saltwater flies are tied on size 4 through 2/0 hooks.

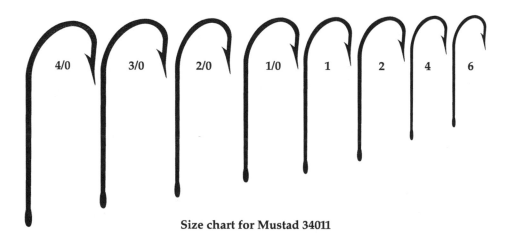

Size chart for Mustad 34011

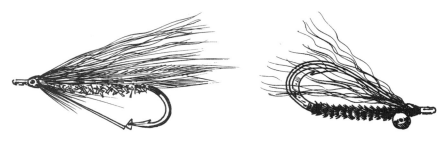

Wire weedguard   **Looped mono weedguard**

Weedless Flies

Weedless flies and bugs are a must when fishing in weedy waters. Most of these have a wire or mono weedguard tied into the fly. Use around any potential snag such as weeds, piers, jetties, oyster bars, or downed wood along a shoreline. Keel hooks and bendback hooks are also possible solutions, using a few strands of mono tied in with the wing to make a weedguard.

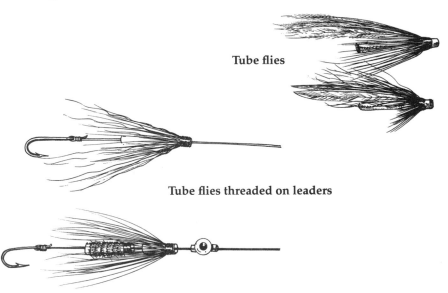

Tube flies

Tube flies threaded on leaders

Tube Flies

Tube flies are becoming increasingly popular. They are not tied on hooks but on thin, stiff plastic or lined metal tubes. The leader is threaded through the tube, then tied to a hook. Separate wings, bodies, and weighted heads allow for a lot of versatility in combining elements of the flies and coping with many different fishing situations.

FLY DESIGNS

Carl Richards, in his book *Prey,* notes that a successful fly must appear alive and lifelike in the water, mimic the natural on the retrieve, feel natural when hit by a fish, and be easy to cast, nonfouling, and durable. Consider all these factors when buying or tying flies.

Surface Bugs

Bugs consist of a body of cork, balsa, or foam plus a tail. Foam bodies are the most durable. Since the fish sees the underside of surface bugs and many flies, it's belly colors that are important, not the pattern on the back. Good belly colors are white, yellow, chartreuse, cream, and black. All your surface bugs should have long-shank hooks for better hooking.

Poppers. Poppers can imitate surface food such as baitfish driven to the surface by feeding predators or a fallen bird. They are not as widely used in salt water as the longer-bodied skippers.

Skippers. Skippers have a face that slopes more sharply than that of poppers, causing them to skip along the surface of the water. Most skippers also have a slightly longer body than poppers, which helps them maintain stability on a fast retrieve. When retrieved rapidly, they simulate escaping baitfish.

Sliders. Sliders are like poppers or skippers in reverse, with the tapered end facing forward. As such, they are ideal fished around structure, along shorelines, or in quiet shallow areas for everything from striped bass to snook.

Pencil Poppers. Pencil poppers are very long, slim poppers that imitate slim baitfish.

Streamers

Streamers are long, slim flies primarily designed to imitate baitfish. Suggestive patterns that simulate only the shape and color of baitfish are popular, although highly imitative patterns with lateral lines, gill plate markings, eyes, and other characteristics are also available. Most are tied on long-shank hooks.

Deceivers. Developed by Lefty Kreh, these are ideal generalized imitations that are highly suggestive of a number of baitfish. They are nonfouling on cast and retrieve, durable, and highly effective. Many variations are possible, but the basic design includes a long hackle tail, tied in at the hook bend and thus nonfouling, and a short, body-encircling bucktail wing.

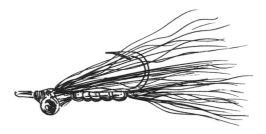

Clouser Minnows. These slim flies designed by Bob Clouser use synthetics or bucktail, are tied to fish point-up, and include weighted dumbbell eyes to make the fly dive.

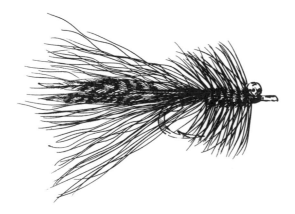

Whistlers. Developed by West Coast angler Dan Blanton, these have a tail of bucktail, a thick full-hackle collar, and bead chain eyes to get deep. As such, they push water and create a large profile to attract big fish. They are similar to Seaducer flies, which also have a full hackle and tail.

Needlefish Flies. Needlefish flies are good for both coastal and inshore species. They are tied with a long, slim wing secured at the rear of the hook shank, the forward part wrapped to imitate a needlefish head.

Specialty Flies
Specialty flies defy easy description. Many are simple and suggestive; others are complex and highly imitative. Their purpose is to suggest a particular prey species, often for fishing a certain situation or for a certain species.

Shrimp Flies. Predators feed on all sizes and species of swimming shrimp. Most patterns include eyes, antennae, the hard carapace, and the legs, or swimmerets. They can be tied tiny to imitate grass shrimp or larger for open-water fishing.

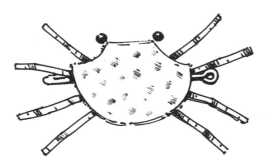

Crab Flies. Crab flies are best tied sideways on a hook, since crabs swim sideways. Floating, slow-sinking, and fast-sinking versions are available in many sizes and colors. Though they're usually thought of for tropical fish, such as bonefish and permit, they are ideal for any coastal species.

Bonefish Flies. Bonefish flies are typically tied on regular-shank-length hooks, designed to ride with the hook point-up and with a wing flared high to cover the hook point. Many colors, designs, and patterns are available.

MOE Flies. MOE flies, short for "mother of epoxy," are made by molding an epoxy body onto a hook, and then adding other materials. They are usually suggestive crab imitations and used for bonefish and permit.

'Cuda Flies. These are similar to needlefish flies, tied long and slim, with only a synthetic tail or wing tied at the bend of the hook shank. Most have the head, wrapped on the hook shank, coated with epoxy for durability.

Stu Apte-style tarpon fly

Tarpon Flies. Tarpon flies are made full, almost like a Seaducer or Whistler, for deep-water fishing, or in the Stu Apte style, with a saddle hackle wing and collar tied on the rear of the hook shank, for tropical flats fishing.

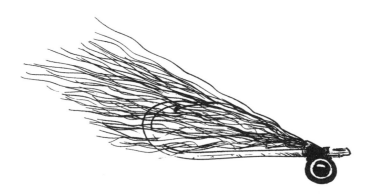

Albacore Flies. Albacore flies are like specialized Clousers, tied with light-colored translucent synthetics and weighted eyes.

On keel hook

On bendback hook

Bottomfish Flies. Keel hooks and bendback hooks are used for bottomfish flies to catch flounder, fluke, grouper, and other fish. The hooks ride point-up, the wing and body tied to imitate basic baitfish.

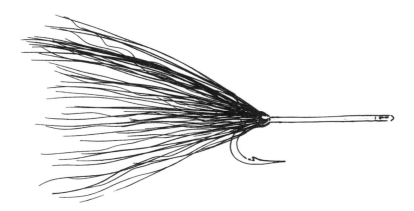

Toothy Critter Flies. Flies for toothy fish such as bluefish, barracuda, and sharks are best on a long-shank hook, tying a simple fly or wing to the shank at the bend of the hook. The bare shank provides a very short bite leader to prevent cutoffs. For larger fish or gulping strikes, include a short wire bite leader.

Chum Flies. Chumming brings the fish to you. Chum refers to ground-up fish or other bait, so an ideal chum fly resembles a chunk of bait. For this, simple rabbit-strip flies are best. Use colors such as white, cream, tan, brown, and red to simulate bait.

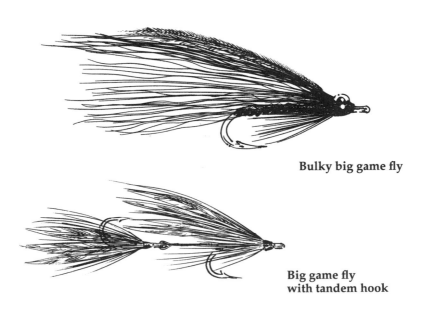

Bulky big game fly

**Big game fly
with tandem hook**

Big Game Patterns and Designs

Flies. Big game flies are tied on standard-shank 4/0 to 7/0 hooks. Often they are tied tandem with the second hook one size smaller, tied point-up to the main hook, using heavy mono or braided wire. Most of these flies are big, bulky, tied in colors to imitate everything from mullet to flying fish to mackerel, and finished with large eyes as a strike-triggering addition.

Poppers and Sliders. Poppers and slider bodies are used to create noise, action, or water disturbance and to keep the offering on the surface. There are several theories about using popper heads. One is that they will make more commotion and thus attract the attention of the fish, but the fish can grab the popper and, by holding it, prevent a good hookup.

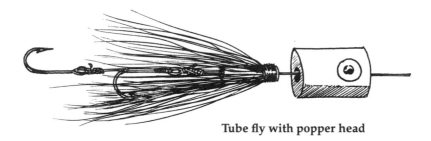

Tube fly with popper head

Tube Flies and Poppers. Flies for big game are increasingly tied on tubes, since these offer a mix-and-match method for body and tail. In a typical rig, a leader is threaded through a tube-popper body and then tied to a large fly. Thus the fly becomes the tail of a large popper. So that the fish will not hold the popper head and thereby prevent a hookup, use soft foam, such as upholstery foam, for the heads. Even though this is an open-cell foam, it will float long enough to make noise and will collapse when a fish hits.

HOOK PREPARATION
Whether tying your own flies and bugs or buying them, sometimes modification of the hook is required. If tying your own, any of the modifications can be done before or after tying. With purchased flies and bugs, check the hooks at home or on the water.

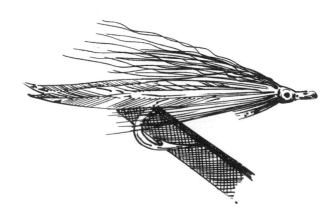

All hooks on all flies and bugs should be sharpened, then checked frequently while fishing. Use a file for large flies or a hone or diamond dust file for smaller flies. Sharpen by triangulating the hook point. To do this, hold the hook securely and work the file or hone at an angle on the inside of the point, between the point and the barb. Do this first on one side, then on the opposite side. Use the file or hone to touch up the outside of the hook point. If you start with a file on a large hook, finish with a diamond hone. If you have trouble holding the hook securely, use a small pair of needlenose Vise Grips or locking pliers.

Opening the bend can be a helpful modification on some hooks, especially keel hooks. Use pliers to bend the hook point slightly outward, no more than 10 degrees, to increase hooking ability.

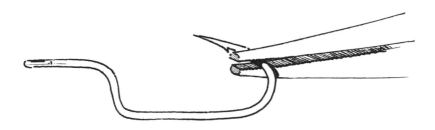

Barbless hooks do not adversely affect hooking, but they make it easier to unhook fish and safer to remove hooks from clothing or flesh. Barbless hooks and barbless flies are readily available. Hook barbs can be bent down with needlenose pliers or removed with a file or hone.

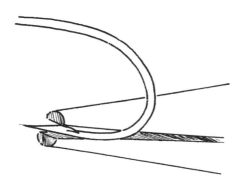

BASIC COASTAL AND INSHORE FLY BOX

Fly Pattern	Colors	Sizes
Lefty's Deceiver	White, black, yellow, green, or grizzly	6–2/0
Clouser Minnow	White, brown, chartreuse, or black	6–1/0
Whistler	White, black, red, orange, or yellow	4–2/0
Sand eel	Black, white, yellow, or tan	4–1/0
Glass minnow	White, yellow, chartreuse, green, or blue	6–1/0
Bendback	Brown, black, white, yellow, chartreuse, or green	4–2/0
Skipper	White, blue, or yellow	1–2/0
Slider	White, yellow, or black	1–2/0
Chum fly	White, yellow, tan, brown, red, or orange	6–2/0

All the above are basic designs rather than specific patterns. Use the pattern or color combinations that simulate local baitfish.

BASIC OFFSHORE FLY BOX

Fly Pattern	Colors	Sizes
Squid pattern	White, tan, pink, orange, or blue	1/0–6/0
Tandem streamer	White, black, orange, blue, green, yellow, chartreuse, or tan	3/0–6/0
Single streamer	White, black, orange, blue, green, yellow, chartreuse, or tan	4/0–7/0
Anchovy	Green, blue, white, or tan	4/0–5/0

Most of the above are used with a foam popper head in front of the fly on the leader, tube-fly style, or incorporated into the hook. Also, tube flies can be used with the individual hook sizes listed.

BASIC TROPICAL FLY BOX

Fly Pattern	Colors	Sizes
Lefty's Deceiver	White, yellow, chartreuse, green, grizzly, or black	6–3/0
Clouser Minnow	White, brown, chartreuse, or black	6–2/0
Whistler	White, black, red, orange, or yellow	4–4/0
Stu Apte style tarpon fly	Red, orange, yellow, or black	1/0–5/0
Sand eel	Black, white, yellow, or tan	6–2/0
Glass minnow	White, yellow, chartreuse, green, or blue	4–2/0
Bendback	Brown, black, white, yellow, chartreuse, or green	8–2/0
Needlefish fly	Orange, red, green, yellow, chartreuse, white, or black	1–4/0
Shrimp pattern	Tan, orange, white, or yellow	2–2/0
Crab pattern	Tan, light blue, light green, or brown	6–2/0
Bonefish fly (Crazy Charlie)	White, tan, orange, or chartreuse	8–1/0
Skipper	White, blue, or yellow	2–2/0

It is important to match local conditions and bait in size, color, and pattern for all tropical fishing. These basic designs can be simulated by a number of patterns.

Chapter 3

Casting

SETTING UP GEAR

Once you have your basic freshwater gear—maybe for bass, maybe for heavy trout, but including rod, reel, line, backing, leaders, and flies—you need to put it all together in a fishable saltwater outfit.

Your first step is to put the line on the reel, but before doing so, make sure to check which way the reel handle turns to retrieve line. Consult the reel manual for the suggested amount of backing that, together with the fly line, will fill the reel. Begin by tying an arbor knot in the backing. Then mount the reel on the rod, with the reel facing correctly, which gives you the rod grip to hold while spooling line, and tightly spool the backing on the reel. Run the backing through a glove to ensure firm spooling, and use your fingers as a "level wind" to spool the line evenly.

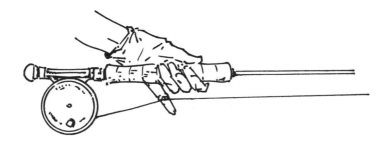

With the backing spooled, attach the fly line with loop-to-loop connections, an Albright knot, or a nail knot. Make sure that any connection is to the back part of the weight-forward line. This is tagged by the manufacturer. If using a shooting head, attach the backing to the running line, then the running line to the shooting head.

Continue spooling until all the line is on the reel. If a leader has not yet been added, do so at this point, using a nail knot, needle knot, or loop-to-loop connection.

Now add the remaining sections to the rod. Double the end of the line and run it through each guide. Do this outside so as not to risk catching the rod in a door or ceiling fan.

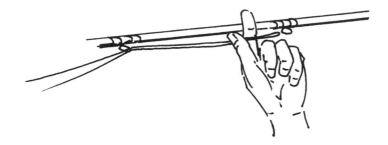

Once the line and leader are out of the rod guides, tie on a small hank of yarn or an old fly *with the hook clipped off*. This will make the leader perform properly during practice.

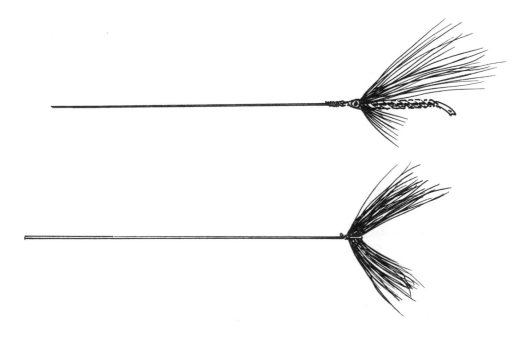

PRINCIPLES OF CASTING

Saltwater fly fishing requires long casts, and the ability to cast well and accurately is a must. To do so, you need to practice. The best practice is on water. Grass will work OK if water is not available, except for a roll cast. Practice when others are not around, particularly pets. Dogs and cats have a thing about catching the end of the line.

Before you begin casting, you need to have a basic understanding of casting principles. First, in fly casting, you actually are casting the line—the fly just goes along for the ride. The thick line provides the necessary weight for casting, and this is why lines of different sizes are different weights to match the power of different rods, just as lures are matched by weight to spinning rods.

Second, the line, when cast, will follow the direction in which you aim the rod. Straight, accurate casts are a result of smooth casting and aiming the rod where you want the fly to land.

Third, you can move the line only if it is straight. Coils or slack line first must be straightened by hand or rod angle before having any effect on line movement or speed. Smooth, straight casting, with no curves, coils, or snaking of the line, is a must to achieve distance.

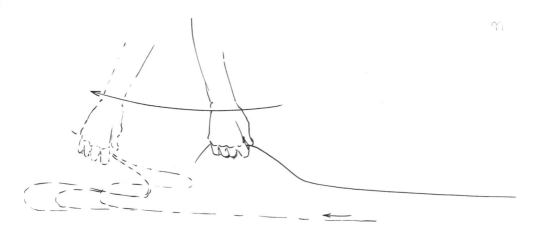

And finally, you can obtain distance only through line acceleration, and this can be achieved only in one of two ways. One way is to pull the line with the hand. Try laying the line out on a lawn and pulling with a hard jerk. The line will snake back at you. The second way to move line is to use the rod. To try this, run the line through the guides, and hold the line securely with the rod hand. With the line in front of you, jerk the rod back or to the side. The line will fly by you as a result of the rod's lever action. These two movements are the basis for every cast.

STANCE
A good stance to push out a cast is important. For this, position your body at a slight angle to the cast direction, the rod arm side slightly back, and the opposite leg extended forward. This allows you to put a lot of shoulder into a cast and to lean into the cast to punch out a long line.

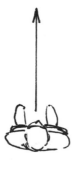

Poor stance

**Better stance
(right-handed caster)**

BASIC CAST

The basic cast involves the hand holding the rod, or rod hand, and the hand holding the surplus line, or line hand. Because there is no single, heavy weight at the end of the line, as with bait casting or spinning, it is necessary to repeatedly cast the line back and forth to obtain distance and accuracy. The cast, though a complete unit, is composed of two separate strokes: the backcast and the forward cast.

Backcast

The first stroke, the backcast, throws the line to your back. Start with the line in front of you, the rod tip low. Hold the outgoing line with the hand gripping the rod. Begin the cast with a sharp and gradually accelerating upward movement, bending and arcing the rod, but stopping the rod movement at about 11 o'clock, assuming that you are facing right (toward 3 o'clock) at the center of a clock face. Do this correctly, and the line will flow back horizontally, the line and leader curling back like a giant hook until it becomes straight. You will also learn to feel the line tug when it straightens. As the line straightens, begin the forward cast.

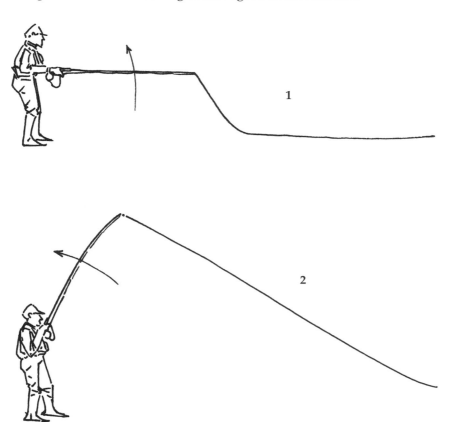

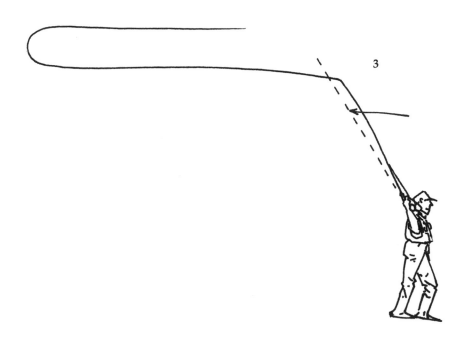

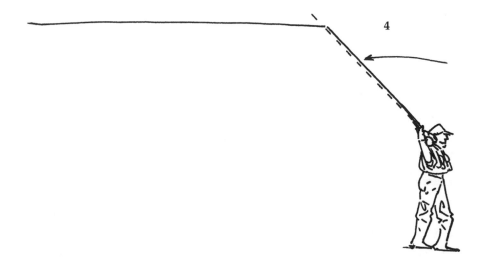

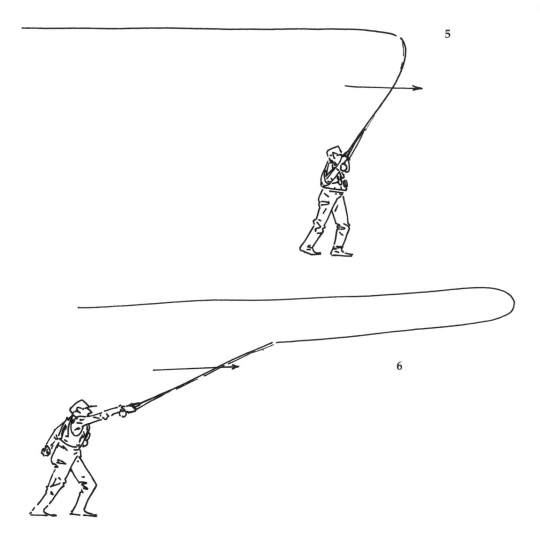

Forward Cast

With the line in back and in the air, begin the forward cast by pushing the rod forward without pushing it down. As your arm pushes forward and the line comes forward, wait until your arm is fully extended, and only then push the rod forward and down in an increasingly accelerated movement. This will cause the line to continue flowing in front of you and ultimately straighten out and land. At this point, the rod should be low, the cast complete, and the fly ready to fish.

Single Haul
All the above was accomplished with the rod hand only, while simply holding the line with the line hand. An improvement on this is to pull on the line in addition to levering the rod to increase line speed. This is a called a single haul and involves holding the line in the line hand, then pulling the line as the rod is levered up and back. The result is two movements in unison: levering the rod back while pulling on the line to increase line speed.

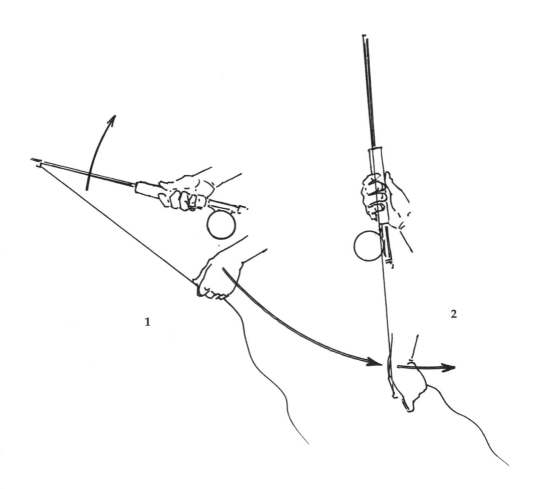

Loop Control

The size of the line loop helps control distance. A wide, open loop will cut distance, both because of the greater air resistance of the increased amount of line and because the line is not propelled properly forward.

Loop size is controlled by the arc through which the rod is pushed on the power strokes of both backcast and forward cast. A narrow arc makes for a narrow loop, which allows distance casting. A wide loop is the result of a wide arc of the rod and does not allow distance or accuracy. This control of loop size is identical on both the backcast and forward cast.

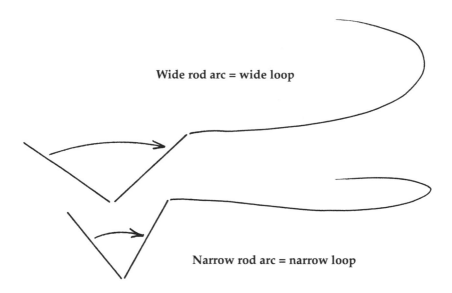

Wide rod arc = wide loop

Narrow rod arc = narrow loop

The Complete Basic Cast

The complete basic cast involves all of the above elements. With the line in front of you and the rod tip low, pull on the line with the line hand as you angle and accelerate the rod upward with the rod hand. Keep this in a small arc to make a narrow-loop backcast. With the line straight on the backcast, push the rod forward, and at the end of this movement, turn the rod over to push the line in a narrow loop, using a small arc of the rod, to propel the fly to the target. Often several casts of the line in the air, called false casts, are made in this way to build line speed and distance and to single out a target.

Angle of Casting
The cast can be made with the rod straight overhead, to the side, or at any angle in between. Most casts are made with the rod at a slight angle, since this is most comfortable. Use a side-angled cast when casting bulky or heavily weighted flies to avoid being hit.

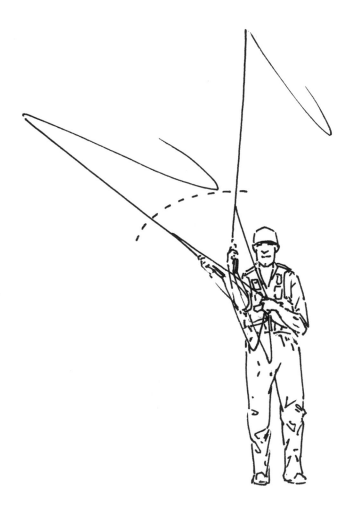

Power and Acceleration

The key to casting is the control of power and acceleration. Power is necessary to get the line to move on the backcast and forecast. Controlled rod acceleration is necessary to use that power properly and to control the cast. Gradually accelerate the rod as you lift up on the backcast to throw the line high and in back of you. On the forecast, accelerate the rod in a forward push before turning the rod in an arc to complete the cast.

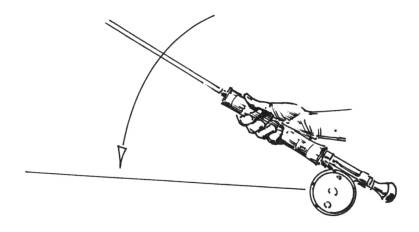

Hand, Wrist, Arm, and Shoulder Control and Use

Grip the rod comfortably. This means a grip almost like that used to hold a hammer. The best grip is with the fingers around the cork grip, the thumb on top or slightly to the side to provide power to push out a long cast.

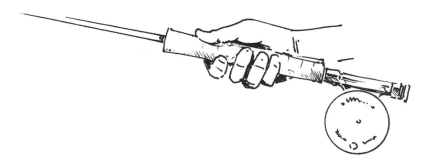

How much arm you should use depends on the length of the cast. Trout fishermen flipping a very short cast use no more than the wrist. Longer casts require some forearm and the elbow joint. Still-longer casts typical of saltwater fly fishing require even more leverage and rod movement by using the shoulder.

DOUBLE HAUL FOR DISTANCE

The double haul is an extension of the single haul, and like the single haul, it allows you to increase line speed and extend casting distance. The single haul involves picking up and pulling back on the line as you raise the rod in an arc to make the backcast. The double haul consists of this plus a similar motion for the forward cast. This second haul starts just as the line straightens out in back and the rod is starting to come forward for the forecast. At this time, pull down on the line so that there is an acceleration of line speed *while the rod is being brought forward and cast*. This can be done during false casts, during the final presentation cast, or both.

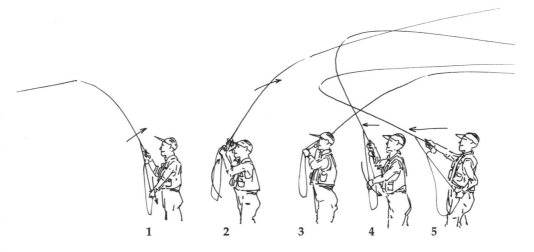

SHOOTING LINE ON THE FORWARD CAST

Extra distance is possible by shooting line on the forward cast. To do this, simply apply more power than necessary to the cast so that the line has extra momentum. Then, as the loop unrolls and the cast nears completion, allow line to slip through your fingers. You can release line by allowing it to run free through a circle formed by your thumb and index finger, or control the final distance with your line hand, stopping the line when the fly reaches the target.

CASTING PROBLEMS AND SOLUTIONS

Casting problems are a result of not doing something correctly. Some common causes and solutions are as follows:

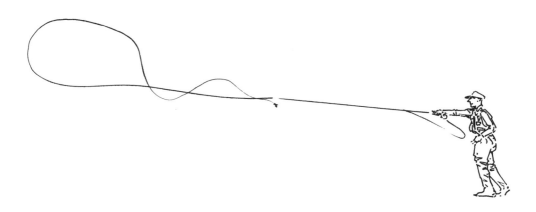

• **Line or leader knots, tailing loops.** Overhand or figure-eight knots in your line or leader are a result of turning over the forward cast too early, pushing the rod forward, or an underpowered forward cast. Each of these requires a different correction. If your cast was underpowered, correct by using more power in the cast. If you are pushing the rod forward too early, try pushing it well forward to power the forward cast, and only then turn it over to cause the loop to unroll. Another solution is to make a sidearmed backcast followed by an overhand forward cast.

• **Not getting enough line speed on the backcast.** This can be caused by too little power or acceleration on the backcast, starting with the rod held high rather than pointed toward the line, or too much slack in the line, in which case you need to make sure that the line is straight so that any power on the backcast picks up the line rather than just removing loops and coils.

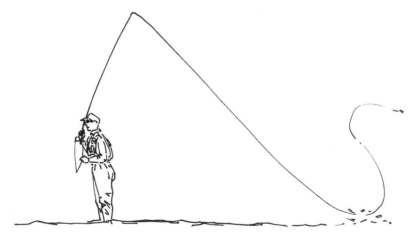

• **Hitting the water or ground on the backcast.** This can be another result of the above mistakes, along with an attempt to correct and get more line speed or control by applying more power to the backcast. If back and at a downward angle, it results in the line or fly hitting the water. The corrections are the same as above. Also make sure that the line on the backcast is thrown high and back, rather than with a curving backstroke of the rod to throw the line downward.

ROLL CAST

The roll cast is rarely used in saltwater fly fishing, but it's useful when fishing from shore where brush and trees line the bank or when up against the shore in a boat but fishing toward open water. Use it to pull sinking or sinking-tip lines from the water to throw the line in the air prior to making a backcast or to roll the line out on the water to make a water haul, which allows the line to be picked up off the water before it sinks again.

The roll cast can't be practiced on land, since the surface tension of water is a must to make it work. Any pond or in-ground pool will work fine. Start by using a floating line. Practice by flipping out some line on the water. Then, instead of holding the rod pointed at the line, bring it straight up and angled slightly behind you. Stop. At this point, the loop of line hanging from the rod tip must be in back of you and behind the rod, the end of the line on the water in front of you. After a short pause, bring the rod down almost like hammering a nail, to cause the rod to roll the line over and out. This lifts the line off the surface and lays it farther out.

This is aided by allowing the line to slip through the guides while raising the rod so that you can get more line out. Another way to do this is to allow some slippage of line on the forward cast to increase roll-casting distance. Don't allow too much slippage, though, or it will kill the cast.

A roll cast can also be done sideways so that the loop of line is in a close-to-horizontal plane to flip a fly or bug under overhanging structure, as when saltwater fishing under a pier or a tree-lined shore.

AERIAL ROLL CAST FOR SINKING LINES

A modification of the standard roll cast is an easy way to pick up sinking lines. Since sinking lines don't float and can't be picked up normally, a roll cast is a must unless retrieving all of the line. To do an aerial roll cast, strip in as much line as you think you can pull from the water. Then make a roll cast, but use an angle of acceleration that will aim the line *up*. This casts the line up and into the air rather than rolling it out on the water. Once the line uncoils in the air, come back smartly with a backcast, followed by one or two false casts to get the line out again to the fish.

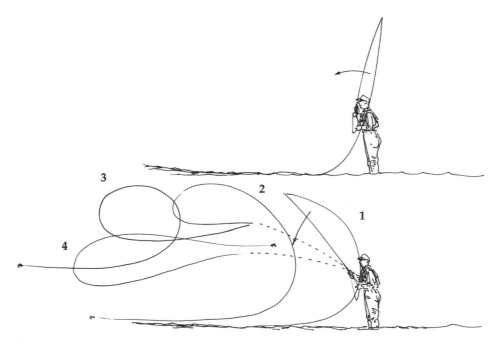

A variation, known as the water haul, is to roll the line up and out onto the water surface, then immediately come back as if picking up a floating line and make the necessary false casts. A water haul can also be done on the backcast to load the rod for a longer, more accurate forward cast. This is particularly effective when the wind is from the back.

CASTING SINKING AND SINKING-TIP LINES

Casting standard sinking and sinking-tip lines is not much different from casting floating lines. There is a slight air resistance and mass ratio difference between the two lines that requires a slightly larger rod angle and more open loop, but assuming identical tapers and identical weights on the proper rod, both floating and sinking lines cast similarly. Where some anglers have to adjust and change is when casting very heavy lines. Sometimes rod sizes suggested by line manufacturers for their lines are much lighter than the rod manufacturers' recommendations.

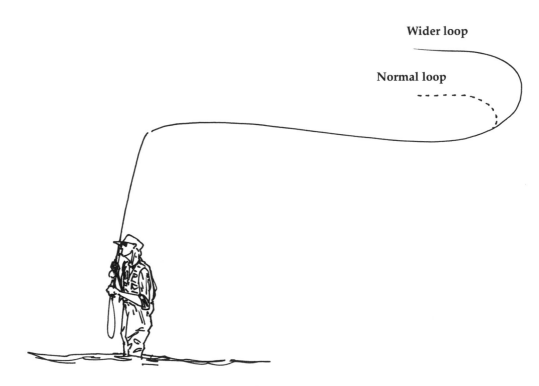

Wider loop

Normal loop

In cases where a rod is severely overlined, whether a floating or sinking line, you must minimize or eliminate false casts and throw one wide-loop backcast and then a wide-loop forward cast to shoot the line to the target.

CASTING IN THE WIND

Fly casting is best when there is no wind. Unfortunately, wind often accompanies fishing trips, particularly in saltwater fly fishing. Though wind can come from any direction, looking at wind from four directions will allow you to make casting adjustments for any wind situation.

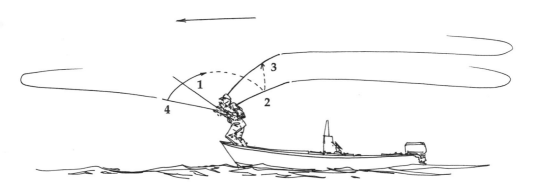

If the wind is from the rear, the best technique is to throw a side-armed backcast so that the line is close to the water, where the force of the wind is less, then turn the rod at the end of the backcast and make a high forward cast to allow the wind to carry the line for maximum distance. Here a wide arc and wide loop of line help to create more surface area for the wind to push the line forward.

With the wind from the front, a regular backcast is possible, but use extra power on the forward cast and throw the line in a low trajectory, because the wind close to the water will be less forceful than that higher up. Drive the cast out low, with a narrow loop and a lot of power. An alternative is to make the entire cast sidearmed and parallel to the water.

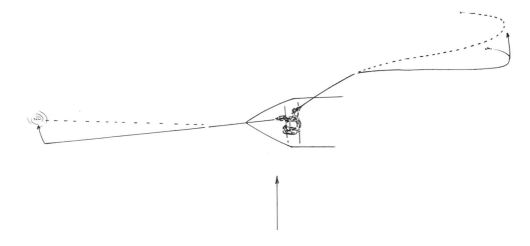

If you are right-handed and the wind is from the left, the main effect will be to blow the line and fly away from you. You will have to compensate for this to hit the target. If you are right-handed and the wind is from the right, it will blow the line and fly across your body and could be dangerous. (Reverse this for a left-handed caster.) To prevent a dangerous situation, cast with the rod held across your body so that the wind will carry the line and fly completely to your left. Another solution is to turn around 180 degrees and make your false casts, then, with the final presentation, turn to convert your backcast into a forward cast and shoot the fly to the target. Always watch out for fellow anglers and boat equipment when changing casts.

SIDE CASTS FOR LOW TARGETS

Snook, striped bass, barracuda, snappers, and other species often hang out under boat docks, duck blinds, shoreline tree limbs, and along the pilings of low bridges. To get a fly to these and similar spots, make a sidearmed cast with the line over the water, making sure you do not endanger other anglers. This allows you to shoot a bug or fly into tight spots that would otherwise be impossible to reach. Another way to do this is to make a normal backcast, then come forward with a strong, forceful, low-angled forward cast to shoot line low and to the target.

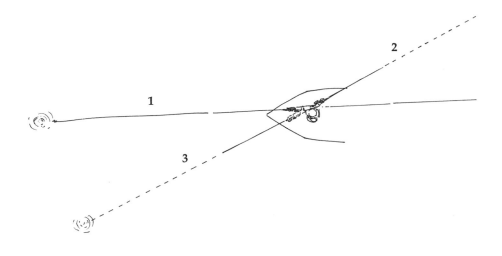

PICKUPS AND REDIRECTION CASTS

One of the advantages of fly fishing is that a bug or fly can be picked up off the water without retrieving all the way back in, as must be done with spinning or casting tackle. This pickup distance will vary with each caster, rod length, and line size. It will also vary with the type of line, since floating bugs with floating line are easy to pick up, whereas sinking or sinking-tip lines require more line retrieved (less line out) and a water haul or aerial roll cast.

This ability to pick up the line also makes it possible to immediately follow through with a second cast after one backcast, two at the most, redirecting the cast to a completely different spot. To do this, first pick up and throw the cast in back of you, but at an angle that is close to 180 degrees from the desired forward-cast direction. To cast to a new target to the left, try to throw the first or second backcast in back of you but to your right. This places this backcast and the follow-through forward cast in a straight plane with the final cast. You won't reach this position precisely, but any backcast in that direction helps. Often you can cast as much as 45 degrees from the original target by perfecting this technique, and do it in one or two backcasts.

On those rare occasions when you hear breaking fish in back of you, glance back to locate the fish, then pick up the line and come through with one backcast to drop the fly or bug in an ideal position. If this isn't possible, make a regular backcast, then a forward cast, at the end of which you turn your hand and twist your body so that your backcast and forward cast are reversed and the rod, reel, and force of the cast are aimed at the spot previously behind you.

SPECIAL CASTING SITUATIONS

That low, forceful forward cast used for a wind from the front is also useful when you have to get a fly out in a hurry and there are birds diving on bait driven up by breaking fish. The low cast keeps the fly in the air a minimal amount of time, reducing the possibility of a gull taking your fly.

If casting to spooky fish, use a high cast, since it allows the fly to drift down to the water rather than slam on the surface, scaring fish. To do this, think of the water as being a few feet higher than it really is and aim high to allow the fly to fall naturally.

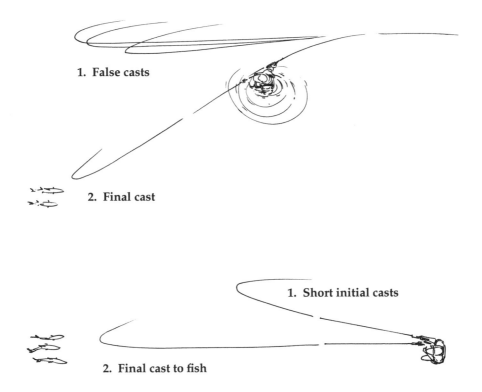

1. False casts

2. Final cast

1. Short initial casts

2. Final cast to fish

If fishing skinny water where the fish might be spooked by the line false-cast overhead, cast to one side of the fish, and only on the final forward cast make the cast to the fish. Another good solution is to make short casts in the general direction of the fish, and only on the last approach make a forceful forward cast and shoot line to reach the fish. When fishing to more than one fish, you can cast only to the near outside edge of the school so as not to put the line over the school and spook the fish. Long leaders help in these situations.

If sight fishing from a boat, you have to be ready to cast immediately. To do this, you must have enough castable line out of the reel, on the deck, or in a bucket or basket, and the fly in your hand. To avoid tangles, make a cast *before* you get to the fishing area, then strip all the line back into the bucket or basket. If you strip line off the reel and into the basket without doing this, the line on the basket bottom becomes the first line out of the rod when you cast or a fish takes, tangling the line. Keep some water in the bucket or basket to prevent the line from blowing around. Hold the fly by the bend, ready to flip it out to start a backcast when a fish is spotted.

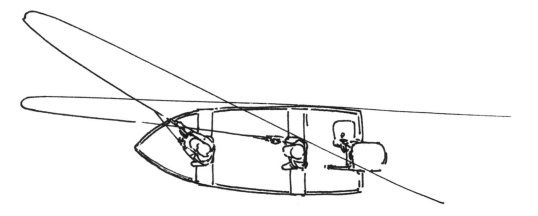

It is unsafe to cast over your partner.

CASTING SAFETY
Always be aware of your surroundings, boat equipment, and other anglers. Anglers may move and put themselves in harm's way. Check on anything that might affect the casting pathway of the forward cast and backcast. Be especially careful on windy days. Be confident of your ability and casting skills to avoid problems and potential accidents, whether fishing from a boat, from shore, or while wading.

RIGGING BOATS FOR FLY CASTING
Boats for fly fishing should be as free from obstructions to your line as possible. Use a basket or bucket for stripping the line. If possible, take down antennas. If fishing from a large boat, store the outrigger on the casting side. Stow other tackle, tackle boxes, and anything else that might catch fly lines. Temporarily cover cleats, anchor chocks, and similar hardware with duct tape. If some items, such as boat controls in the stern, can't be removed, cover with a large square of netting to prevent line tangles. Add pinch-on sinkers around the rim of the net to prevent it from blowing around.

Put duct tape over cleats to prevent stripped line from tangling on them.

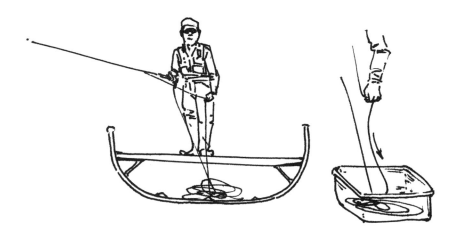

The ideal small boat for fly fishing has front and rear casting platforms, often pulpit style with rails to keep the caster in place in rough water. Rod racks under the gunwale must be long enough to hold 9-foot fly rods. Depth finders are a help in locating fish, as are GPS units to chart the course to fishing grounds or to mark a wreck or reef.

Chapter 4

Basic Fishing Techniques and Retrieves

BASIC FISHING TECHNIQUES
Preparations
Before making the first cast on any saltwater fly-fishing trip, be sure that the rod is assembled properly, ferrules seated firmly, reel secured on the reel seat, line through all the guides, and drag properly set. Preset drag (straight reel drag) is a function of the tippet test. Using a scale, set the drag at 10 to 20 percent of the tippet test—heavier only if fishing structure where you might have to prevent a fish from cutting off. This setting, usually about 1 to 3 pounds, might seem light, but additional drag is added by rod angle, guide friction, palming the reel, and water resistance.

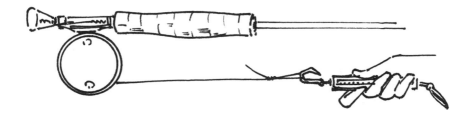

Casting

If blind casting, try to make each cast to the best possible spot, based on structure and current, and plan for successive casts to cover more water or a different depth of water. In some cases, this means starting casts at the outside edge of a weed line or current eddy, around a piling, or near another area likely to hold fish, then gradually working to the better spots.

If fishing on a tide where only one cast is possible before drifting out of range, make each cast to the best possible spot. If sight fishing, drop the fly some distance away, and then move the fly so that it acts natural and the fish seems likely to intercept it. This is particularly important in skinny water, since fish can be spooked by being lined or surprised with a fly. Exceptions to this would be some fish with poor eyesight, such as sharks and redfish, where you should drop the fly closer and to one side, within their visual area.

Working the Fly

If blind fishing, work the fly through the cast as naturally as possible, and stay prepared for a strike. Keep the rod tip low and pointed toward the fly or line. Vary the retrieve constantly, attempting to simulate bait. If working a minnow imitation, this might be a constant darting, jerking action to mimic their nervous actions. If working a crab fly, a dead drift or very slow retrieve is best—crabs don't dart and weave. For shrimp flies, use a regular darting motion to imitate their jerky movement.

If a fish appears interested but does not strike, vary the retrieve. Often a *slightly* faster retrieve makes it appear that the meal is escaping, triggering a strike.

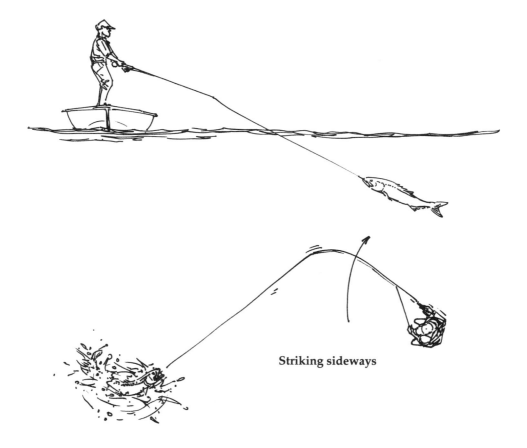

Striking sideways

Striking

There are several ways to strike fish. One is to keep the rod tip pointed low and toward the line. As the fish takes the fly, pull on the line while keeping the rod tip pointed toward the fish. In other cases, it's best not to strike until the fish turns and you can feel its weight. In still other cases, it's best to feel or watch the fish take the fly, then, while holding the line, move the rod sharply sideways to strike. Do not use the tip of the rod to strike; it is too weak. Instead, with a tight line, pull on the line as you lever the rod horizontally so that you are using the butt strength of the rod to seat the hook.

On hard-mouthed fish, strike several times. You can raise the rod slightly to strike with the powerful butt section. With sharp hooks, most fish will stay on. If you can see the fish and it is facing toward you, often a slight pause to allow the fish to turn or take the fly deep helps. If the fish is going away from you or is at right angles to you, the chances of hooking it in the corner of the mouth are much greater.

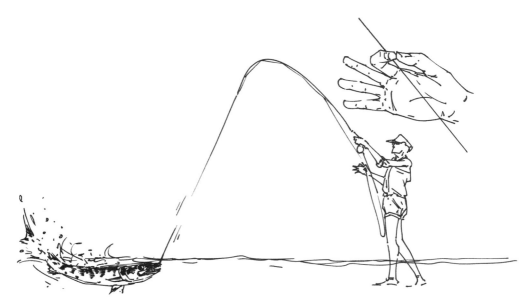

To prevent tangles as a fish starts its initial run, allow line to run through fingers formed in an O.

Immediately after the Strike

Saltwater fish can be big, and your actions immediately after striking are important. You might just as easily sink a hook into a 20-pound striper as the 2-pounder you thought you were going to catch, or a 50-pound shark instead of a 15-pounder. After the fish hits and you make a few strikes, you may not be able to strike again, since the fish will be hauling for the far shore. You must release the line after striking any big fish, or something will break. Allow the line to run out of the stripping basket or off the deck and through your fingers. Make your line-hand thumb and index finger into an O to help clear any tangles. Hold the rod high and pointed toward the running fish; tangles will more easily clear with maximum space between the deck coils and the rod. If the fish takes all the stripped line, line will then start running off the reel. When this occurs, make a slight lunge and slightly bow the rod as the line starts off the reel to compensate for the increased inertial torque as the reel drag starts. Let the fish run.

You can help to sink the hook, even in these situations, by allowing the line to run through your fingers or off the reel and, without holding the line, levering the rod back and sideways to increase pressure in a movable strike or slip strike.

BASIC RETRIEVES

Basic retrieving is done with the line hand, not by manipulating the rod. Jerking the rod to move a fly or bug may tangle the line around the tip end, create slack in the line, or position the rod at a poor striking angle. In all cases, keep the rod low and pointed toward the fly. If the line develops a severe sideways belly due to current or tide, do not aim the rod at the fly or bug, but keep it straight with the line for better striking.

In some cases, you should begin the retrieve even before the fly or bug hits the water. In other situations, the fly or bug must be allowed to drift or suspend first, perhaps settle on the bottom, or maybe drift with no retrieve at all. With breaking fish, begin the retrieve with the fly or bug in the air so that the fish is immediately confronted by a moving meal. The same applies to some tropical feeders, such as barracuda. For bonefish, cast so the fly will land to intersect the feeding approach of the fish. Let it drift to the bottom, and begin a retrieve only as fish approach.

When fishing deep, pause after the cast to allow the fly to sink. Often a countdown method is best, counting down to different depths on each cast until hitting a fish. This allows repeatability of retrieves. For this to work with several companion anglers, the sink rates of the lines must be identical or must be adjusted for by countdown time.

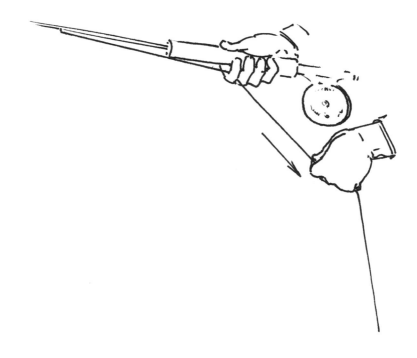

Surface Retrieves

Pause. If fish are not actively feeding, a pause as the fly or bug lands, and between other retrieve patterns, often works to entice the fish into a second look. Pauses suggest injured bait that has to stop and rest, often triggering strikes.

Twitch. A twitch is nothing more than a little jerk—a slight movement of the fly or bug that makes it look alive, spastic, yet injured.

Jerk. Make pronounced jerks of the fly or bug when fish are more actively feeding or to vary the retrieve pattern with a different movement. Jerks on topwater poppers can either provoke a violent strike or scare fish away, so use them carefully. Repeated jerks are ideal for working a topwater popper over breaking fish, because the repeated noisy action can prompt explosive strikes.

Swim. Swimming motions are nothing more than a continual movement of the fly by stripping in line. Since you can strip continuously only with a two-handed retrieve, this is usually varied with a pause, along with twitches, jerks, and so on.

Pop. Popping bugs and skippers are best worked with strong popping motions, making sharp jerks to cause the bug to pop and gurgle, but not enough to move it any distance. Ideally, you want the maximum noise with the minimum forward movement.

Touch and Go. Bugs or flies dropped onto the surface and immediately picked up repeatedly can cause fish to strike in anger. The method is to cast a short-enough line so that you can drop the fly or bug onto a target area and immediately pick it up for a backcast and drop it again, doing this several times in quick succession. After several of these, drop the bug or fly and give it a standard pop, jerk, or twitch. Often fish are by this time primed to take it. This retrieve is best used only as a last resort and after trying some of the other retrieves, and only when you are dropping the fly or bug onto known fish or near structure that you strongly suspect holds fish.

Underwater Retrieves
Underwater retrieves of flies can be accomplished with a floating line if fishing only slightly under the surface, with sinking-tip lines for fishing deeper, and with full-sinking lines or fast-sinking shooting tapers or even lead-core lines for fishing very deep.

Pause. Pauses are necessary to allow an underwater fly to sink to a predetermined depth, settle on the bottom of a shallow flat, stay in position until spotted by a feeding fish, or to break up the action of the fly and make it seem like injured bait.

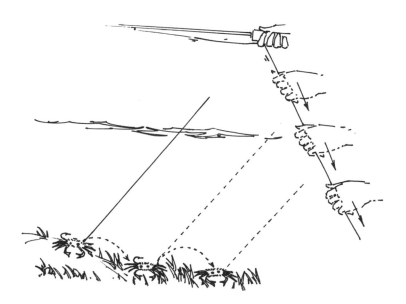

Hop. Bottom-fished flies for bonefish, flounder, sea bass, and others can be hopped along to simulate the action of shrimp or crabs. This works best with weighted flies that return to rest on the bottom. It is also important to make only the slightest twitches so that the hops are measured in inches and not feet. Too long a hop will pull a fly out of the feeding range of fish.

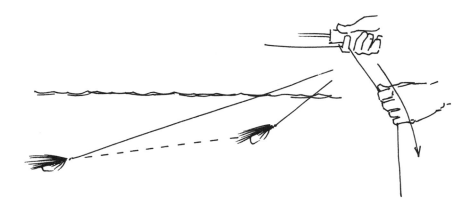

Jerk. Strong jerks after a pause will often trigger fish to strike, because a jerk will simulate a rapid movement of the bait and an apparent attempt to escape. Short jerks are good when fishing streamers and squid patterns, since they simulate erratic baitfish or the jerky propulsion of squid.

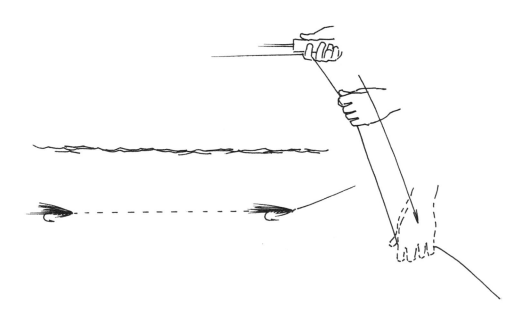

Swim. Swimming a fly by moving it in a smooth motion is usually used where such a retrieve can simulate a fish lost from its school. Often this retrieve is best when interspersed with other retrieve methods.

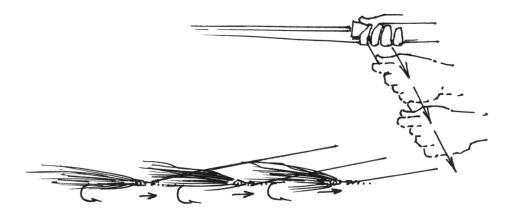

Twitch. A twitch can simulate a slight movement of bait and has the advantage that when it's done right, it rarely moves the fly more than a few inches. Mix it with other retrieve methods for best results. It's ideal when a fly is suspended, since it will make the fly jump to the side and appear to be wary or injured bait.

Drift. Tides and currents allow fishing highly suggestive or imitative flies without any movement, letting them float as the current takes them. This is best done with shrimp, crab, or minnow patterns on moving tides around fish-holding structures such as bridge pilings, jetties, buoys, or channel markers. It's also good when fishing chum flies in a chum line.

Unusual Retrieves

Fishing a Floating Line and Sinking Fly. A floating line and sinking fly will get a fly down slightly and will control the depth. The depth achieved will depend on the weight of the fly (weighted flies will sink faster than nonweighted), length of the leader, and speed of the retrieve. Too heavy a fly will pull the line down and negate depth control; too fast a retrieve will plane the fly up. Heavily weighted flies are difficult and jerky to cast. This method is ideal when fishing over submerged grasses or snags that might otherwise catch the fly.

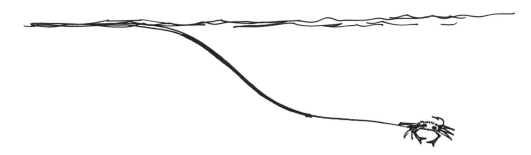

Fishing a Sinking-Tip Line and Sinking Fly. A sinking-tip line and sinking fly allows you to fish deep and stay there—something difficult with fast retrieves when using a floating line and sinking fly. Sinking-tip lines also allow easier pickup and casting, since it's easy to retrieve rapidly to plane the sinking portion of the line to the surface, then pick up the line as you would a standard floating line. Sinking-tip lines vary in sink rate and length of the tip, thus allowing depth control. Even with a sinking fly, use a short, 3- to 4-foot leader to avoid suspending the fly.

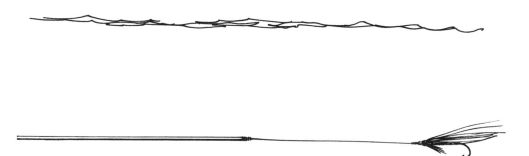

Fishing a Sinking Line and Sinking Fly. Full-sinking lines are harder to pick up off the water—you'll need to use an aerial roll cast—but they do allow you to keep a fly deep throughout the full retrieve. Slow-sinking lines are good if fishing around floating grass and flotsam that might catch on a floating line. Sinking lines vary from slow sinking to very fast sinking and, as with sinking-tip lines, should be used with a short leader.

Fishing a Sinking-Tip Line and Floating Bug. With a short-tip sinking-tip line and a long leader, you can fish a floating bug so that it will float at rest and dive on retrieve as the angle of the leader and the sink rate of the line pull it down. This can often be a deadly combination, particularly when working a bug or diver over a deep flat or bar, where the strange action will attract fish. Vary the depth and degree of the bug action with the leader length.

Fishing a Sinking Line and Floating Bug. A sinking line will take a small floating bug down and will hold it above submerged grass or a snaggy bottom. This is good in situations where the sinking line will scare up bottom bait to act as chum.

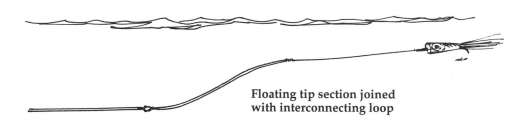

**Floating tip section joined
with interconnecting loop**

Fishing a Sinking Line with a Floating Tip Section. A new technique
is to fish short lengths of floating line interconnected by loops to a sinking
or sinking-tip line. These can be made or purchased with a floating line
and interconnecting floating, intermediate, medium-sinking, and fast-
sinking tip sections. Lengths of 2, 5, and 10 feet are best. This allows you to
get the line down, perhaps chum by moving bait, and fish higher in the
water column to avoid snags when using flies that would otherwise sink
or suspend. Use a short leader.

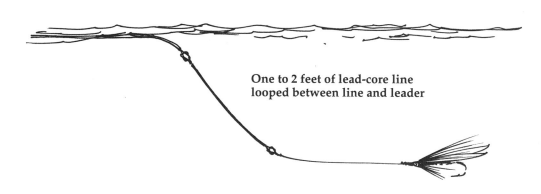

**One to 2 feet of lead-core line
looped between line and leader**

Adjusting Lines with Lead-Core Sections. Lead core sections, about a
foot or more long, with loops in each end, allow connecting to the end of
the line and above the leader as well as in the middle of the leader. With
them, you can convert any floating line into a mini sinking-tip line.

Two-Handed Strip

Some fish require a fast, continuous retrieve. Barracuda are a good example; they usually won't hit a slow fly. This retrieve requires a different technique. One method is to make the cast, place the rod grip between your knees, and then use both hands to continually strip in line as fast as possible. A second method is to place the rod under your arm and make the same retrieve. Pull straight down on the line with one hand while supporting the line with the other. Constantly changing hands and pulling down allows an easier fast retrieve than trying to pull back. Sometimes it helps to stabilize the rod by sticking the tip into the water. When a fish hits, strike, then grab the rod handle with one hand while using the other to help the line flow through the guides as the fish runs.

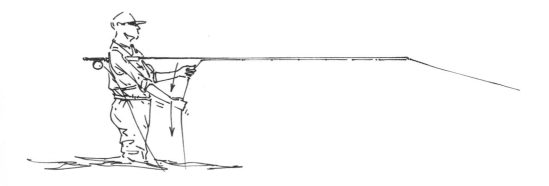

Cast ahead of moving fish so you can adjust presentation and sink rate of the fly to intercept them.

SIGHT FISHING

Sight fishing is casting to fish that you can see or see evidence of. It might be fishing a flat where fish are cruising and feeding or casting to visible fish on structure, to visibly migrating fish, to schools of nervous bait, or to roiled water caused by fish mudding the bottom. It involves casting to fish that are generally holding or moving in a predictable direction. This allows you to adjust flies and tackle and cast to present the fly on an intersecting path with the fish. With breaking fish, the action is so frantic that you are not casting to individual fish, and the techniques are different. It is necessary to understand the fish, how fast and deep they are moving, and how they are feeding. Choose an outfit with the right type and sink rate of fly so that the fish can easily spot it.

To sight-fish effectively, cast so that the fish will see the fly in a position where it will want it. Unless you're using a floating bug, you must know the sink rate of the fly. Check this alongside the boat *before* spotting fish. When you sight a fish, be aware of its speed, distance from you, and direction of movement so that you can drop the fly in the right spot.

In some cases, you might actually see the fish. This can occur in clear, shallow water and is most prevalent with cruising bonefish, tarpon, permit, and similar species. In other cases, you might only see evidence of the fish, such as nervous water, dorsal fins of fish, tailing fish feeding on shallow flats, or wakes of large, deeper fish. If you spot a dorsal fin or tail, but glare prevents you from seeing the entire fish, calculate the fish's size and cast far-enough forward so that the fly will intersect with the front end of the fish, not the dorsal or tail. Wakes from fish are often slightly behind the fish, depending on water depth, so cast far-enough forward.

With some fish, such as bonefish, you can drop the fly ahead of them and allow it to rest on the bottom until they are in the area, moving it only then to trigger a strike. With other fish, or in open, deeper water, cast far enough to begin a retrieve that will place the fly at the right depth, speed, and position for the fish to spot it and want to hit it.

Avoid scaring fish by hitting them with the fly or line or dropping the fly too close to the head of the fish, behind the fish, or in a blind spot immediately in front of the fish.

Sight fishing from a boat gives you added height above water—a distinct advantage. However, the sight of the boat or your higher profile, or the boat drifting over them, can spook fish. When fishing from a boat, stay aware of the boat, the location of your fishing companions, and your casting pathway in relation to them and to the position of the fish.

Wading places you lower in relation to the water surface and makes sight fishing more difficult. It does have the advantage of creating a lower and less visible profile of you to the fish and allows you to cast in any direction, assuming that other anglers are not within range.

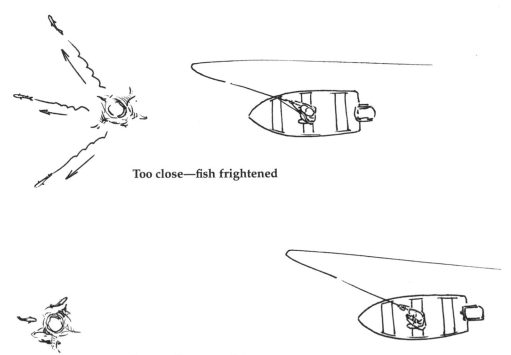

Too close—fish frightened

Proper distance—fish unaware

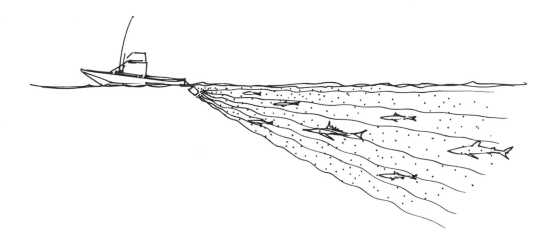

CHUMMING

Chumming is a method of attracting fish to you. It is easy to do from an anchored boat by spreading chum, or bait, over the side. The rocking movement of the boat spreads the chum through the water and creates a downcurrent chum slick, which attracts fish. You can grind up chum (often oily fish such as menhaden, although any bait or fish can be used) with an onboard electric grinder and spread a watery mix of this over the side. Other chum can include shrimp bits, crushed soft-shell clams, or live anchovies or sardines. All chum has to be distributed constantly to maintain the chum slick. Usually only short casts are necessary with a sinking-tip line and chum flies. Chum flies can be simple rabbit-strip flies that resemble chunks of fish flesh or large streamers and Deceivers if using live bait.

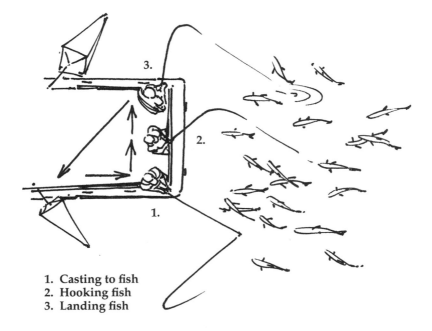

1. Casting to fish
2. Hooking fish
3. Landing fish

The best technique is to make a right-handed sidearmed cast from the port/transom corner of the cockpit. This prevents you from catching outriggers or antennas, although if possible, it's best to place outriggers in an up or stored position and lower antennas. After you've had a turn, move to the starboard side to allow room for another fly caster. Three or more fly anglers can fish this way on most charter boats. The best fishing is from an inboard engine boat so that the engine won't interfere with casting or controlling line. Boat courtesy while chumming requires short lines on the deck to prevent tangles, moving out of the way after casting your fly into the chum slick, and staying on your side of the boat to lead the fish away from the chum slick and those not yet hooked up.

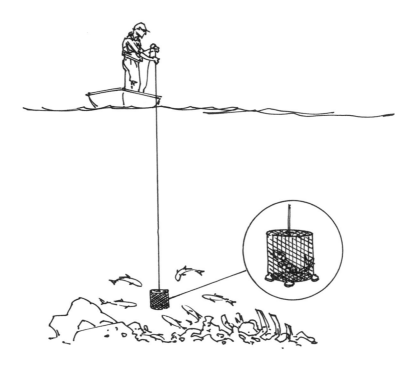

You can chum fish such as amberjack up from the bottom by using a marked line tied to a weighted mesh, or hardware cloth, chum bucket closed at the top and open at the bottom. Add chum to the bucket, invert it in the water, with the open bottom down and closed top up, to sink to close to the bottom, then pull up on the bucket to release the chum. The weight hanging from the open end of the bucket will keep the chum in place while the bucket sinks. Repeat this, releasing bait higher and higher each time (that's the reason for the marked line), until you attract fish to casting range. Continue to chum the surface to hold the fish in place.

Chum for bonefish or other flats fish by cutting up shrimp or conch and tossing bits of it into a channel while at the edge of a flat in a small boat. You can also work from farther up on the flat if the tide or current will sweep the chum into the channel holding the bonefish.

You can chum with a bag of ground chum while shore fishing, provided that there is enough current to spread the chum slick. Do not do this while wading—it is dangerous, because the same chum slick that attracts your quarry may also attract sharks.

Land the fish quickly for release. Some fish might take the fly deep. If you can't easily get the fly out with a disgorger without causing bleeding, cut the leader a foot away from the mouth and release the fish. (Leaving a length of leader outside the fish's mouth allows it to more easily expel the hook.) To avoid deep hooking, consider circle hooks for chum flies.

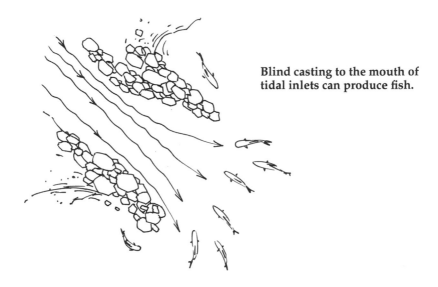

Blind casting to the mouth of
tidal inlets can produce fish.

BLIND CASTING

Blind casting is casting to the water rather than to spotted fish. Cast to structure under conditions conducive to attracting fish. For coastal species, such as stripers, seatrout, or snook, any structure is good on a running tide. For inshore fish, such as cobia or dolphin, cast around flotsam, buoys, and piers.

Vary your casts until you locate fish. Fan-cast by casting in an arc all around you or to cover a structure area or shoreline. If fish are deep, use the countdown method, making several casts to the same spot and varying the count to reach all levels of the water column.

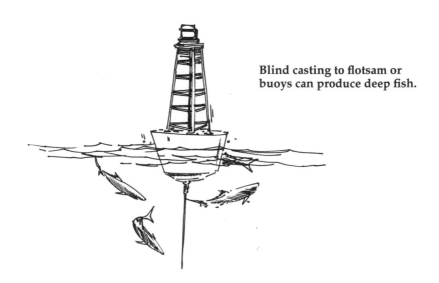

Blind casting to flotsam or
buoys can produce deep fish.

Casting to breaking fish

BREAKING FISH

There is no greater excitement in saltwater fly fishing than casting to breaking fish. Often the noise sounds like rain on a tin roof. To add to the confusion, gulls and terns often dive on the frantic, broken, and bleeding bait driven to the surface by game fish. It can be frantic for anglers trying to fly-cast into the mess without snagging a wing or having a gull snatch a fly in midair.

This type of fishing requires a ready-rigged outfit, right down to the fly. Most important in fly selection are the size and color. Try to match the bait as closely as possible. Make sure that you have the right tippet—a short bite leader for bluefish, for example.

Smooth but rapid casting is necessary, since schools are up and down constantly. Make your casts low and only as far as necessary to get to the fish; long, high casts are likely to hook birds and lose time.

Begin the retrieve with the fly still in the air, and retrieve in short, rapid jerks to simulate fleeing bait and feeding game fish. If you get a strike and miss, keep right on retrieving; don't skip a beat, for more fish will follow. It's not uncommon to have several missed strikes before hooking up, often right at the boat.

If bait is breaking or birds are diving but there is no visible sign of game fish, they might be deep. In these cases, cast, then count down before beginning a retrieve to fish deeper. This technique is good if you are catching only small fish, because bigger fish often are on the bottom of a breaking school. A sinking line, short leader, and the right fly can get to these fish. Don't retrieve while waiting for the fly to sink; this may trigger hits from smaller fish.

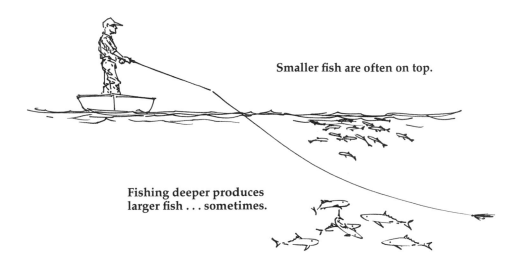

Smaller fish are often on top.

Fishing deeper produces larger fish . . . sometimes.

One of the best ways to locate breaking fish is to glass the horizon for choppy water or diving birds. Birds do several things that can tell you about fishing. Birds sitting on the water are resting, meaning that there are no fish in the area. Birds flying aimlessly or in a straight direction are moving to a new location. Birds hovering overhead may be signaling bait underneath, but the bait is too little or too deep to reach. Birds dive-bombing the surface are actively feeding on bait driven to the surface by game fish. Birds often dive differently on different fish. They are often less frantic diving on feeding stripers than when over the chopped-up bait created by a frenzy of bluefish. In the southern oceans, large man-o'-war birds, or frigatebirds, follow and signal game fish.

Hovering birds
May be bait or fish

Flying birds
No bait or fish

Diving birds
Bait and usually fish

Resting birds
No bait or fish

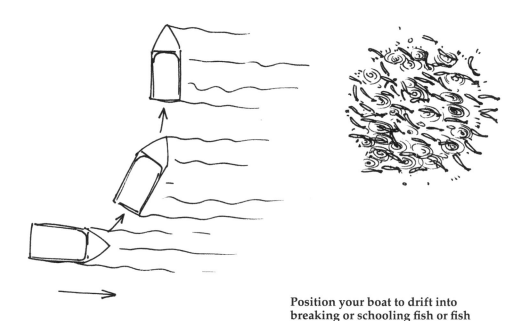

Position your boat to drift into breaking or schooling fish or fish moving toward you.

Once you spot breaking fish, approach them carefully. Do not run your boat through the school. Kill your engine before getting too close to the school. If the school is staying up and moving and there is little tide or wind, position your boat a cast length ahead of the school. Often the school will move, surrounding you with breaking fish.

If there is a strong tide, current, or wind, and the school does not show signs of moving, position your boat on the upcurrent or upwind side of the school, whichever is stronger, and allow the boat to drift into the feeding frenzy.

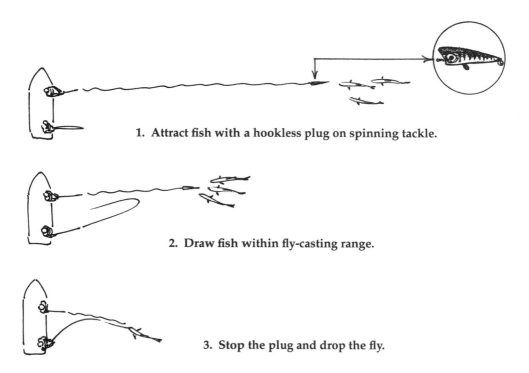

1. **Attract fish with a hookless plug on spinning tackle.**

2. **Draw fish within fly-casting range.**

3. **Stop the plug and drop the fly.**

TEASING FISH AND TROLLING

Teasing fish is a method of attracting fish with a hookless lure or bait, then catching them on a fly. Inshore species such as stripers and bluefish can often be teased within fly-rod range. Use a heavy spinning rod and large surface plug with the hooks removed. With a fly-rodding partner ready with a big popper, cast the plug and rapidly work it back to the boat. Fish often can be seen chasing and striking the plug, which they can't catch because it lacks hooks. Once within fly-casting range, the fly caster drops a bug right on top of the churning plug. Now stop the plug and immediately work the popper, at which point the fish will transfer from the resting plug to the noisy popper.

The same technique can be used with bait or lures to bring amber-jack up off reefs and tease barracuda and cobia away from structure. With subtle modification, this is a great technique for a wide variety of game fish.

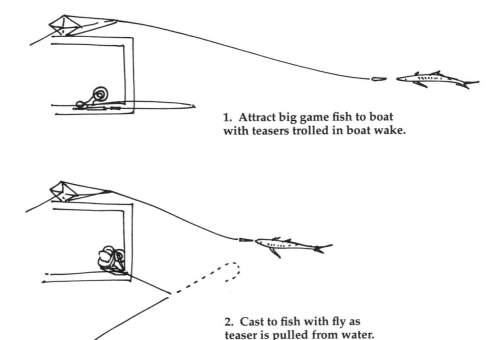

1. Attract big game fish to boat with teasers trolled in boat wake.

2. Cast to fish with fly as teaser is pulled from water.

Big game fishing for wahoo, billfish such as marlin or sailfish, dolphin, sharks, and tuna necessarily involves trolling, as blind casting from a dead boat would be like trying to find a needle in a haystack. This requires three persons: the captain, a mate to control the teasers, and the fly rodder. While the captain runs the sportfishing boat at trolling speed, which varies under different conditions for different species, the mate trolls artificial teasers or bait from one outrigger, opposite the fly rodder's position. The other outrigger should be kept in a raised position. Troll two teasers maximum, trailing from the starboard side of the stern for a right-handed fly rodder.

When a fish shows up, the mate moves the teasers in closer to bring the fish to the boat's stern. The fly rodder stands in the port/transom corner and prepares to cast. With all but one teaser in, the fly rodder casts while the mate swings the lure aboard, and the captain shifts into neutral. It is important to have the fly land at almost the same time that the teaser is pulled from the water so that the fish doesn't lose interest. The fish, having lost the teaser it was trying to eat, will attack the next thing it sees, which is the popper or fly. This is one time you should throw the fly just a little in back of the fish, so that the fish will swing and take the bait going away, reducing the possibility of its landing in the cockpit if it jumps.

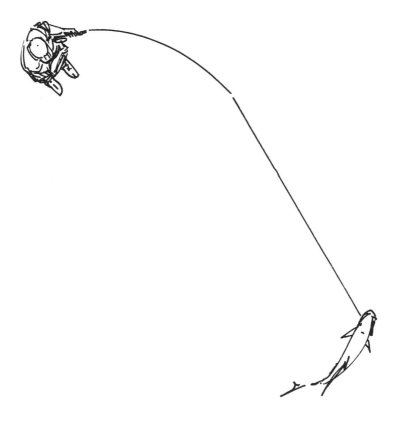

FIGHTING FISH

Fight fish by letting them wear themselves out against the drag, realizing that fishing drag is a combination of reel drag, guide friction, rod angle, and water resistance to the line. Do not try to work fish with a high angle of the rod. Instead, keep the rod at about 30 to 45 degrees to the water. The best way to fight big fish is with the rod almost parallel to the water and working with sideways pressure to move the fish and turn its head. This also helps keep the fish from jumping, which is when most fish become unbuttoned. Equally important, turning the head of a fish to keep the fish at right angles to the direction of the line will minimize contact of the fish with the line or leader. With big fish, this can be a problem, since swimming tails and abrasive scales can snap or abrade leaders or line. This is most serious when fish are swimming directly away from you.

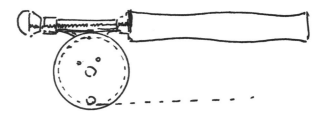

A full 4-inch reel with the drag set at 2 pounds

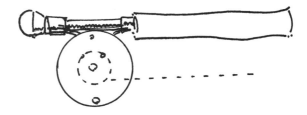

**With half the line stripped off the same reel,
the drag increases to 4 pounds.**

Drag Control

Even with the drag set properly, adjustment is sometimes necessary during the fight because of the shrinking working arbor size of line peeling off the reel. A drag set at 2 pounds on a 4-inch-diameter full reel is increased to 2.66 pounds when the functional diameter of line shrinks to 3 inches, and to 4 pounds at 2 inches.

Added to this is the increased drag through the friction of the guides, angle of the rod, and drag of the fly line and backing pulled through the water. What started as a workable drag may wind up snapping a tippet. To prevent this, back off the drag as a fish makes a long run, then slowly increase the drag again as the fight comes closer. On most reels, with a lightly set drag, you can increase pressure on the fish by holding the rim control, releasing as required. Never increase the reel drag over the original setting.

If a fish jumps, do not pull back with the rod, as this could easily break the tippet. Instead, drop the rod and point it at the fish. Drop the rod tip into the water to lessen the line shock on the fish, or thrust (bow) the rod toward the fish to decrease stress.

When fighting fish from a boat, keep the rod at a low angle or close to horizontal; this will more easily turn its head and move it. Do not pump straight up with the rod, particularly on boats with overhead structures. You may snap the rod if it hits something or if the leader tippet breaks or the hook pulls out, causing the rod to fly back sharply.

With large fish, have your partner raise outboards and pull in any overboard items that might catch on the line, such as chum bags and buckets, bait buckets, anchor rope, staked boat poles, and trolling motors. Lead fish away from the motor. If the fish heads toward the motor or runs under the boat, stick the rod straight down in the water—down to the grip, if necessary—to help clear line from the lower unit or prevent it from abrading on the hull. Move the rod underwater past the prop or bow and bring it up on the opposite side of the boat to regain line.

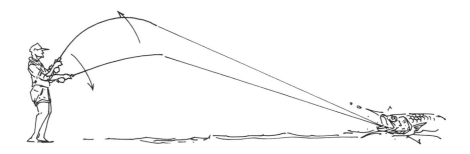

PUMPING

Pumping is a method of gaining line. To do this, raise the rod, using it as a lever. At the top of this levering action, drop the rod while spooling line on the reel. Do not rapidly drop the rod, since this will create line slack, which a fish can use to escape, or the line might get wrapped around the tip-top, causing the tippet to break. Once you have gained line on the reel and the rod is again horizontal, repeat the process. If the drag starts to slip while doing this, do not adjust it; use your hand on the palming rim of the spool to prevent slippage. Should a fish lunge or make a run, release the line while bowing the rod to eliminate shock and breakage.

LANDING FISH

Proper landing of fish depends on whether you're fishing from shore, wading, or boat fishing; the size and species of fish; and whether you're keeping or releasing the fish. If shore fishing, lead the fish with the rod into shallow water with a gradual sloping bank. It is easy to get a beaten fish into shallower water than it would normally tolerate. Once in shallow water, grab the fish in back of the head, holding it securely to remove the fly. Do not do this if the fish has teeth; instead, cut the leader or use a long-handled dehooker.

Use the same techniques when wading. For small fish, it often is possible to partly immobilize the fish by holding it against your leg or by tucking your rod underneath your arm and holding the fish with one hand while using the other to remove the fly. Small fish can sometimes be lifted by the belly or side, partially and temporarily paralyzing them for handling and hook removal.

When boat fishing, lead the fish to the boat, making sure that the inside of the boat is clear of rods and other gear that might get damaged or wet during the landing, and that there are no bumpers, chum bags, or anchor lines outside the boat in the landing area.

With any fish, make sure that it's tired before you land it. It will often be on its side, close to the surface, head out of or near the surface. Use the rod at a side angle to lead the fish to you.

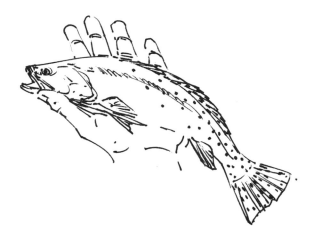

If the fish is small, such as white perch *(above)*, lift it by hand and hold it securely around the middle to remove the hook. If it's a spiny fish *(below)*, run your hand over the fish from front to back to keep the spines safely down while grabbing it. Holding the fish belly-up tends to disorient the fish and keep it quiet during hook removal.

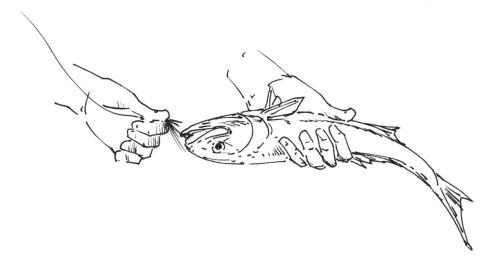

For larger fish that do not have teeth, such as stripers and snook, you can lip them and lift by the lower jaw *(opposite page)*, but be careful of the sharp gills on snook. Note the position of the fly or bug. If it's in one side of the fish's mouth, grab the other side for safety. Lift straight up, and do not bend the jaw if you plan to release the fish, as this may injure it.

Fish with teeth, such as sharks, barracuda, or bluefish, must be handled with care. Land toothy fish with a net, mechanical lip gripper, or gaff. Use a gaff in the body only if keeping fish for food.

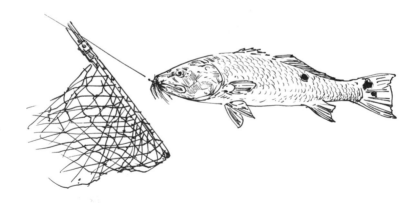

To net a fish, lead it headfirst toward the net, with the net frame at least halfway submerged in the water, the bag flowing away from the fish. As the fish enters the net, sweep the net forward and raise it immediately to contain the fish. If you're in a boat, lift the net up and hold the bag against the gunwale until the fish quiets down.

Lightweight lippers made of plastic can be used for fish up to several pounds. Larger lippers that will weigh the fish are also available. Often the fish will have its mouth open as you are ready to land it. Grab the fish with the lipper by the lower jaw and lift straight up.

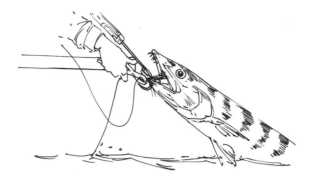

To gaff a fish for release, use a short hand gaff and gaff through the lower jaw, going from inside to outside. This allows you to pin the fish against the gunwale of the boat to remove the fly without hurting the fish. If not pinning the fish to the boat, it's easier to gaff through the outside of the lower jaw.

If keeping fish, use a long-handled gaff to body-gaff the fish. The best method is to hit the fish about in the middle, through the upper, muscular part of the body; hitting a big fish in the stomach might tear it and require a second gaffing. Before gaffing the fish from a boat, open the fish box so that with one easy swing of the gaff and fish, you can drop the fish in the box, jerk the gaff out, and slam the lid. To remove the fly or cut the leader, wait a few minutes until the fish is dead.

For big game fish, such as marlin, an experienced mate will handle the fish, usually by grabbing the bill, then cutting the leader or working the fly free quickly to release the fish. If you must grab the bill of a billfish, do not have the bill pointed toward you at any time or you may be injured if the fish should lunge. Other fish are usually handled by cutting the leader or using a dehooker to remove the fly.

CATCH-AND-RELEASE

Catch-and-release is the practice of immediately releasing fish so that they can live to fight another day, or to make other fish for your children to catch. The best catch-and-release technique is to land the fish rapidly so that you do not tire it out and cause a fatal buildup of lactic acid in the muscles. Using tackle that is too light can kill fish this way.

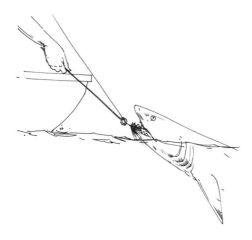

Always release fish while they're still in the water to give them the maximum chance of survival. Do this by unhooking the fly and allowing them to swim away. Hemostats, long-nose pliers, or a mechanical dehooker is ideal for this. For toothy fish, such as sharks or barracuda, it's necessary to use a long-handled dehooker made for this purpose. If the fly is deep, don't try to retrieve it. Cut the leader leaving 1 foot outside the fish, then release the fish.

One good way to assure fish survival is to hold the fish by the side of the boat or in the net after landing to allow it to recover. Then remove the fly or hold the fish up for a quick photo by a buddy before releasing it. If a fish is exhausted, first hold it by the lower jaw or body and move it back and forth to force water through the gills to revive it. It will swim away when it's ready.

Chapter 5

Where and How to Find Fish

Many factors affect finding fish and effectively fishing for them. Each species has its own preferred habitat, food, temperature range, and migration patterns, and each reacts differently to tides, structure, temperature gradients, salinity, depth, and seasons. Learn as much as possible about the fish you plan to seek. Even though fly fishing is different from other fishing methods, you can benefit by listening to other anglers, tackle shop owners, and fisheries biologists to learn more about the fish you seek.

TIDES

Tides are important for many reasons. Along the coast, they constantly flush water, waste, food, and bait, with two complete tides that culminate with two high tides and two low tides. Two cycles are completed in about twenty-five hours. Tides create currents and chop that mix oxygen in the water, bring food to waiting game fish, change the water level to allow feeding in areas that are too shallow or exposed at low tide or too deep at high tide, and help maintain constant water temperatures. The result for the fly fisherman is that tides allow optimal fishing opportunities in different parts of a given waterway as they rise and fall.

Tides are affected by a number of factors, but mostly by the moon. The earth rotates on its own axis every twenty-four hours, and the moon revolves around the earth once every twenty-eight days. This results in two tides daily, one when a given body of water on the earth and the moon are closest, and the other when that body of water is 180 degrees away, on the opposite side of the earth.

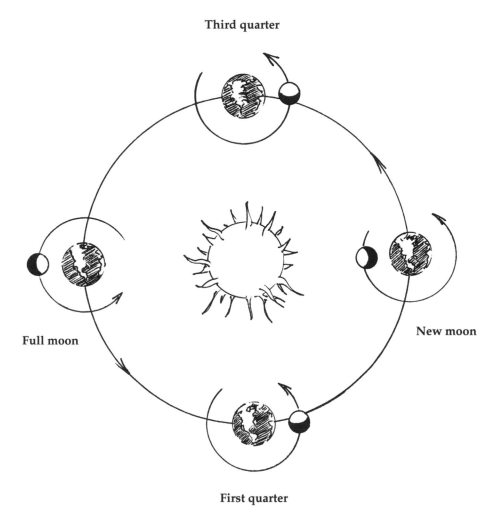

There are tides in which waterflow up and down is greater than normal, called spring tides, and ones with less fluctuation, called neap tides. Spring tides occur on the new and full moons. Neap tides occur on the first- and third-quarter phases of the moon.

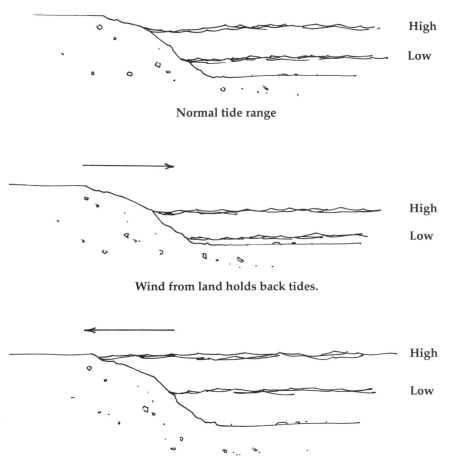

Normal tide range

Wind from land holds back tides.

Wind from ocean increases tide range and water depth.

Wind, other currents, and coastal river flows also markedly affect water movement. Wind can hold a tide back or push it forward. A wind blowing offshore as a tide is going out will hasten that outgoing tide and push more water than the tide alone would move. This can affect fishing and access: Shallows that can normally be boated on a falling tide can become exposed and leave your boat high and almost dry until the next incoming tide. A wind blowing offshore against an incoming tide can hold that tide back and keep the water low. A wind blowing from the ocean will increase an incoming tide and the ultimate height of the water level, and hold back an outgoing tide and keep it higher than normal. To further complicate things, the force of the wind and length of time it blows will have an effect on tidal levels and movement, with additional effects based on whether these are neap or spring tides.

Tide tables for coasts are available from the National Oceanic and Atmospheric Administration (NOAA). Most seaside tackle shops also provide simple tide charts for their area, and many print annual tide tables showing the high and low tides throughout the day for a given point. This is important, since highs and lows farther inland or offshore, or in different parts of a bay or estuary, will be at different times. This is especially true in bay, inlet, and tidal river areas, where tracking a tide is more direct and easier. Most tide charts will also list plus or minus times for a number of areas that are added to, or subtracted from, the basic chart.

SPOTTING FISH

Spotting fish is critical where you are casting to specific fish or fish schools. Fish can be spotted by seeing them through the water, watching for flashes they make underwater while feeding, noting water disturbances that they or bait make, watching feeding activity of birds and marine mammals, or noting the activity of other fish species with which game fish mix. Spotting game fish involves using all methods and techniques available to you, particularly being aware of activity or water movements that somehow look different or out of place.

Oil Slicks

Fish feeding on oily bait such as menhaden will create a surface oil slick. These areas often have a fresh fish or cucumber smell. If fish are not visible, this can mean that they are feeding deep or that they have fed and left the area, leaving the slick behind. Look uptide, upwind, or upcurrent of this slick for activity. Spots like this are always worth a check on the depth finder and a cast or two. Oil slicks will usually be calmer than the surrounding water and have an oily or glassy sheen.

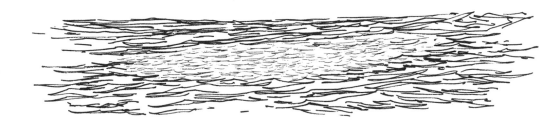

Nervous Water

Nervous water or ripples can be caused by bait or fish moving in shallow water or just under the surface in deep water. They might be feeding, migrating, or searching for food. Because fish are skittish in such situations, cast to the outside edge of such an area, and then gradually fan-cast into the ripples. Ripples or nervous areas look different from the surrounding water.

Tailing Fish

Bottom-feeding fish, such as redfish, bonefish, or permit on flats, will often have their tails out of the water as they search for food head-down in shallows. This can occur with almost any fish that frequent shallow water, particularly shallow-water bottom feeders. Watch such movements to determine the direction of the fish or school (often there are several or more fish). Cast forward of the leading edge of a school to prevent spooking the fish.

Mudding Areas

Mud or puffs of sand or marl can indicate feeding fish stirring up the bottom. Casts to such areas can get a fish or two before scaring the school. Mudding can also be caused by other feeding species followed by game fish, such as bonefish feeding on tidbits left by rays.

Birds as Signals

Gulls, terns, and other coastal and ocean birds diving onto bait often indicate game fish driving bait to the surface. Gulls are better than terns, because terns are smaller and are satisfied with smaller bits of bait that may only be left over from a previous breaking school of fish, and they often indicate smaller fish. The key to using birds as fish locators is that the birds must be actively diving, not just flying by or hovering.

Shadows and Shapes

The key to finding fish on sunny days in clear, shallow water is to know how fish appear in shape and shadow under fishing conditions. Because of water refraction and the angle at which you spot fish, most appear slightly larger than they really are, and also farther away. Compensate for this when casting. Most fish, when viewed from the side, also appear thinner than they really are.

Freshwater trout fishermen learn that they cannot see trout on the bottom because of the dark camouflaged back and sides but can spot the flash when fish roll to take nymphs. The same is true in salt water, where bonefish are best spotted by looking for the shadow they make or their gray, ghostly appearance in the water. Learn to look through the water into the depths or on the bottom of shallow areas, rather than just scanning the surface. To detect fish, look for movement and differences from the natural bottom or water appearance.

STRUCTURE
Structure is something natural or artificial in the water that attracts and holds game fish. Successful fishing can often be had around various forms of structure.

Jetties
Jetties, or breakwaters, are artificial structures that extend out into the water to provide protected water for ships, channels, or swimming. They can be made of many materials, including large rocks or chunks of concrete. Inshore fish, such as stripers, bluefish, seatrout, grouper, barracuda, kelp greenling, opaleye, sea bass, and flounder, are often found around jetties.

1. From jetty

2. From boat

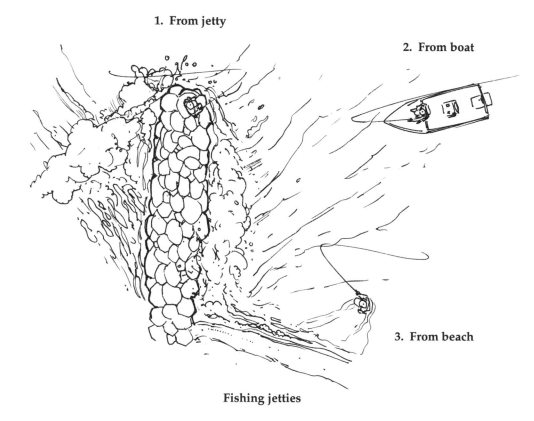

3. From beach

Fishing jetties

Fish only from jetties with flat tops; those with jagged tops or random rockpiles are highly dangerous. Jetties can also be fished from a boat or while wading nearby. If fishing from a flat-top jetty, use rock creepers or cleated boots to cut through the algae. It is important to have a stripping basket, because line caught between rocks will be abraded, cut, or caught. Waders and a waterproof parka are necessary on wet jetties. Floating lines are best, even if fishing sinking flies; otherwise the wash around the jetty may catch lines. You'll need a long-handled gaff to lip or body-gaff fish caught from jetties. But unless there is minimal wave action and the jetty top is close to the water surface, do not try to land fish or retrieve flies. A better way to land fish is to allow the onshore wind to belly the line and pull the fish to the beach, while you walk to shore to land the fish safely.

Be careful if wading, since currents can wash holes into an otherwise flat, sandy bottom. Keep a reasonable, safe distance away from the jetty. Use a stripping basket. Floating or intermediate sinking lines are best. An intermediate sinking line is ideal if fishing where the rocks can't grab the line, and a floating line is best if fishing at the jetty base. Use a heavy leader tippet, as it is necessary to immediately turn a fish away from the jetty to fight in open water. Usually, the wash and pounding waves make it difficult to see leaders.

If boat fishing around a jetty, keep the engine running, for tide, current, and waves can rapidly draw a boat into the rocks. Have someone man the boat controls at all times. In some jetty areas, it's possible to anchor, but use enough anchor rope to hold, and do not anchor anywhere it is prohibited, in dangerous areas, in narrow channels or inlets, or where there is extensive boat traffic.

Coral Reefs

Coral reefs are actually colonies of living reef animals. As structural reefs are built up over time, they also attract other sea life—animals, plants, sea weeds, and small reef fish—all of which attract larger game fish, such as barracuda, grouper, hinds, snappers, and sharks.

Some coral reefs reach the surface at low tide, but no reef should be walked upon, since this will destroy them. Fish from a boat unless the reef is close to shore and you can reach it with a long cast. Anchoring can hurt a reef, so to avoid damage, try as much as possible to drift over coral reefs, or use a Global Positioning System (GPS) to occasionally reposition. A depth finder, often keyed to a GPS unit, is also a must to show the shape and structure of the reef to determine how best to fish it.

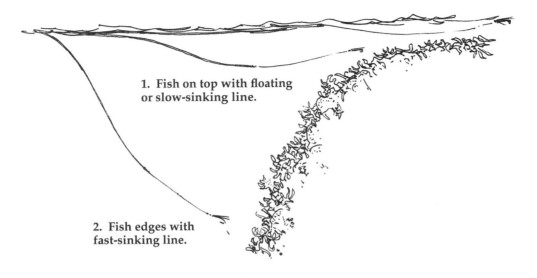

1. Fish on top with floating or slow-sinking line.

2. Fish edges with fast-sinking line.

Fishing coral reefs

How you should fish a coral reef depends on the type of reef. Since reefs are typically tropical outcroppings, they can be fished on top using a floating or slow-sinking line, sometimes even a fast-sinking line if the top of the reef is deep. Make sure the line will not reach the reef, where it can snag. If fishing alongside a reef with a sharp dropoff, you can use anything from a floating line to a fast-sinking line, depending on the quarry and depth sought. Medium- or fast-sinking lines are best only if you know that you are fishing relatively open water next to a reef wall.

Choose tackle geared to the expected size of the fish, perhaps even heavier. If fishing deep-sinking lines to get on the bottom next to a reef with big flies for grouper, use a long, heavy leader and heavy tackle, since hooked fish immediately head for the coral. The long, heavy leader will better hold the fish and will protect the line from getting pulled into the reef and becoming abraded. Barracuda are frequent reef dwellers, so a short length of braided or solid wire as a bite leader is a must.

Artificial Reefs

Artificial reefs are man-made and can be such things as sunken ships, cars, buses, concrete blocks or rubble, or chained-together rubber tires. They are generally attractive to and hold deep-water fish such as grouper, croaker, and sea bass.

Most artificial reefs are too deep for practical fly fishing. Many, such as sunken ships, have a lot of line-catching snags. The best are those made of rubble or cast structures that attract fish but have minimal snags. Most are indicated by GPS or loran coordinates and are marked with permanent buoys.

Because most artificial reefs are deep, use full- and fast-sinking or lead-core lines, along with short leaders and weighted flies. Make long casts, and count down to get the fly to the fish. Use a slow retrieve to keep the fly deep throughout the retrieve.

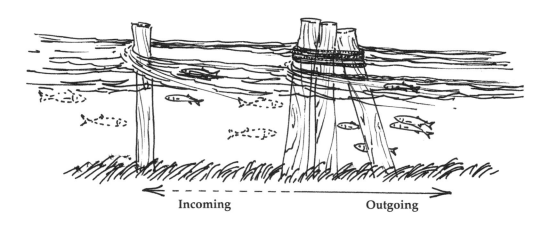

Incoming   Outgoing

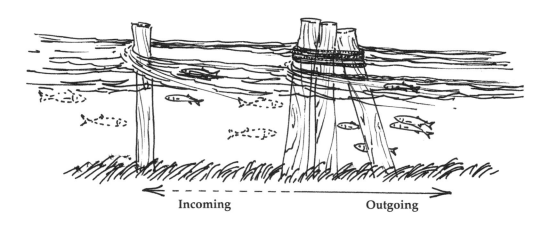 Fish position on outgoing tide

 Fish position on incoming tide

Pilings

Pilings are used for breakwaters, to mark channels, and as supports for bridges, piers, and docks. Since they are coastal and inshore structures, they are subject to tides and ideal for much fishing. The downcurrent or downtide side of pilings provides quiet water where fish can rest and dart out to take food and is often the best spot to fish, but this changes with each tide. Typical catches are stripers and seatrout in the north, snook and tarpon in the south.

Cast where the fly can be intercepted by fish. This might mean casting upcurrent of the piling and letting the fly or bug wash down past the structure and fish. In the case of large pilings or groups of wood pilings, use as short a line as possible, and cast to the still wash in back of the piling. Use a high rod to reduce line drag and work the bug or fly through the quiet water. Try this first at the tail of such a wash, gradually working closer with successive casts, until casting right in back of the pilings. It is often possible to take more than one fish from such structure; fishing the tail first is less likely to spook other fish. Use floating or sinking lines, based on the depth around the piling and the species sought.

Weed Beds

Weed beds can vary greatly in salt water. Long, thick, and ropy strands of kelp are found off Catalina, milfoil and eelgrass in brackish water, weeds around and over coral in the Tropics, and turtle grass on tropical flats. They all hold prey and bait, making them ideal for feeding game fish. Weed beds reduce the current flow a little, creating protected water and ambush areas for game fish while producing the oxygen necessary for fish life.

Weeds are fished differently, based on the type, but in all cases, you have to be able to fish without catching weeds on the fly or bug. This means weedless flies or bugs, using one of several weedguard styles available. With turtle grass on flats, you might need a weedless fly, or if the grass is intermittent, you may be able to snake a fly back between weed strands. Long, ropy weeds such as kelp are best fished straight up- or downcurrent, casting between the strands, giving you a clear path to retrieve the fly, and making it possible to get the fly deep. The best approach is to cast parallel to the edge of the bank, working a fly at different depths to attract fish in the weeds.

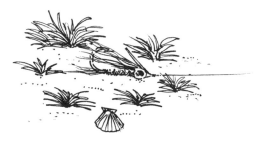

Point-up fly for bottom fishing

Mono weedguard for swimming through weeds

Mangroves

Mangrove thickets and islands can be found in tropical areas, with their knees and arcing root systems creating warrens of protected waters for baitfish and game fish. Snook, mangrove snappers, grouper, barracuda, ladyfish, sharks, and tarpon may be found there.

Fish hide under mangroves, making accurate casting mandatory. Because of the shallow water, floating or slow-sinking (intermediate) lines are best. High tides allow fish to hide farther under mangroves, and low tides can push them to the outside edges. The best fishing possibilities are on the shady side, where fish will often cruise in front of the mangroves rather than hiding in the back recesses. Poppers and shallow streamers are best.

Fish hide deep in mangroves at high tide.

Fish stay on the edges of mangroves at low tide.

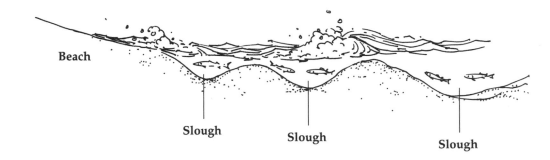

Sloughs

Sloughs are basins of deeper water, found in sandy areas, often between the beach and a coastal bar. They create water deep enough to hold and shelter game fish, protected by the beach on one side and the shallow bar on the other. Game fish such as stripers, false albacore, and bluefish cruise through such areas, which also hold bottom fish such as sea bass, flounder, and redfish.

Use a sinking line to cast as far as possible over a slough, allow the fly to sink, then strip back slowly to keep the fly deep. Fishing is particularly good at cuts between bars that create a mini inlet for fish.

Bars

Sandbars are usually parallel to the beach and offshore from a few to several hundred yards. They are visible by the water breaking over the bar, with swells forming on the shore side of the bar before the water breaks on the beach. Some bars are so shallow as to be visible all the time or visible on a low tide. They afford protection to fish, which are often found on both the outside and inside of a bar.

Bars are really a continuation or border of a slough and can be fished the same way at the same time. If possible, cast a fly or bug up onto a bar—visible or submerged—and retrieve the fly into the deep water on the inside of the bar and in the slough area.

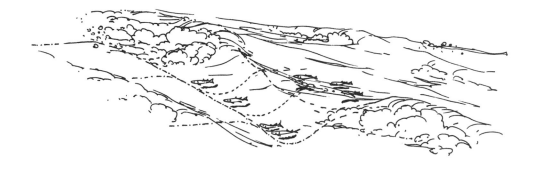

Cuts

Cuts are areas between bars that allow for easy movement by fish between the ocean and the protected waters of a slough. As such, they are ideal places to fish, since they often hold resting fish or fish moving toward or away from a slough.

Fish cuts similarly to sloughs and bars, casting into the deeper water of the cut and allowing the fly to sink, then stripping slowly back through the slough. Because cuts are deeper than the water over the bar on each side, use a sinking or sinking-tip line and imitative streamers. Be careful when fishing cuts, as these areas can cause riptides that are dangerous to waders and swimmers.

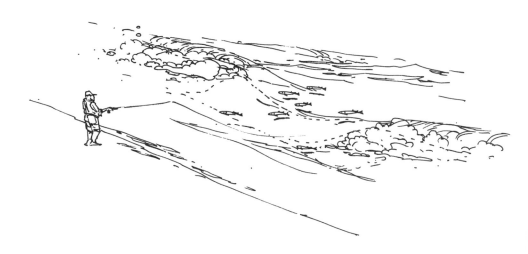

Flotsam

Flotsam is anything floating on the surface, often debris washed into the water or from shipwrecks or lost cargo. Flotsam provides shade and protection and attracts bait, making it ideal for holding fish. It often holds offshore dolphin or inshore cobia and is well worth a cast.

The best method is to get up- or downcurrent and cast close and parallel to the long side of any floating debris. Work poppers, then try sinking flies such as Deceivers. Once you hook a fish, especially so with dolphin, others may stay in the area as long as one is kept in the water. Do not land a fish until you have a second hookup.

TEMPERATURE GRADIENTS

Temperature gradients often are associated with offshore currents or inshore river, power plant, or bay tidal flows. They are important, because one temperature range will hold fish, and such gradients serve as an edge that holds bait and attracts game fish. Temperature gradients can't be seen, although sometimes there is a difference in water color, turbidity, or waves, and sometimes they are suggested by rip lines. Surface-water thermometers on boats can be used to locate temperature gradients. Often birds or small baitfish will indicate activity on one side of a temperature edge. Fish these edges using poppers if shallow fish are present, baitfish imitations on deep-sinking fly lines if blind fishing.

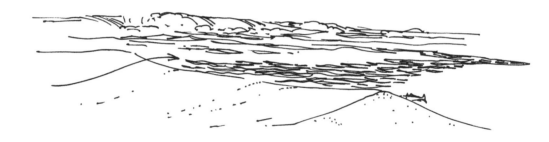

RIP LINES

Rip lines, or tide lines, are those lines where different currents or tides meet. They are often visible on the surface as lines of foam, weeds, or other debris and mark the edge or seam of different water masses. Weeds marking these rips hold bait that attracts fish.

Fish by casting parallel and close to the rip, using poppers, slow sinkers, and Clousers to fish all levels of the water column. Fan-cast to bring the fly through these edge areas.

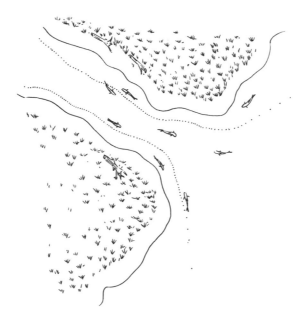

FISHING INLETS

Inlets are narrow necks between the open ocean and shorebound bays, coves, rivers, and backwater areas. A lot of food and water washes back and forth through inlets with each change of tides. Often the currents are strong and difficult to fish unless you find breaking fish or fish sinking lines near protected jetty areas or breakwater walls.

Inlets are the paths through which sportfishing and commercial boats travel from shore to the ocean. Most are marked with buoys for this and may have Coast Guard stations nearby. It is generally unsafe to anchor in an inlet or between marker buoys, and it is illegal to tie to any buoy. If you are not anchored, you must give way to any boat under sail. Narrow inlets are treacherous areas for small boats, particularly when the tide and wind are pushing in opposite directions. Use caution based on water conditions, your boat size and type, and fishing possibilities.

If the inlet is large and the water isn't too rough, you might find breaking schools of fish. In the mid-Atlantic and northeastern areas, breaking schools of stripers and blues are not uncommon in inlets, with seatrout often found near breakwaters and jetties. If blind casting in a running tide, cast upcurrent with a sinking fly and sinking or sinking-tip line, and retrieve just fast enough to maintain fly contact. This allows the fly to sink to its maximum depth. If deep structure shows on the depth finder, fish over or around the structure, working downcurrent in the quieter water and buffer area. Inlets can include various kinds of structure, such as pilings, oyster bars, or jetties; use the methods outlined above to fish them.

FISHING FLATS

Flats are shallow waters with a flat, even bottom. They are often thought of as tropical, but they're found in other areas as well. A flat can be just a few acres to hundreds of acres in size, bordering land or a deep-water dropoff or channel. Most flats are deep enough to hold fish—at least at high tide—and many are shallow enough to wade, although Mark Sosin and Lefty Kreh, in their book *Fishing the Flats*, describe flats as water less than 12 feet deep.

Some flats might be high-tide flats, others only low-tide flats. A high-tide flat will be exposed or too shallow on a low tide, and a low-tide flat might be too deep on a high tide. Flats also vary in temperature during the day and with weather conditions and seasons. Temperature-sensitive fish will flock to flats or avoid them based on this. A shallow flat, particularly one with a dark bottom that will absorb heat, warms far more quickly than surrounding water. This may attract fish seeking the warmer temperature or may send fish into the deeper, cooler channels if the water becomes too hot. You have to know the flat and the fish to know when and how to fish them.

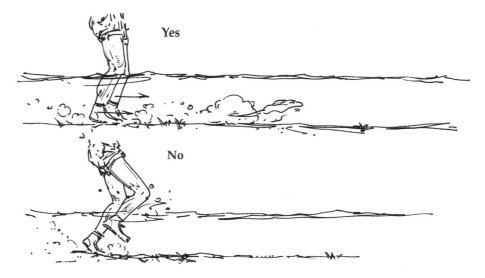

Yes

No

Shuffle feet when wading to move stingrays and avoid stepping on them.

Flats can be fished by wading, if they are shallow enough, or by boat. Wading slowly is ideal to intercept feeding schools of fish. A boat is necessary on deeper flats. Much flats fishing is sight fishing, and you'll need polarizing glasses, a dark-brimmed cap, and a knowledge of what you're looking for, depending on the fish species. In the Tropics, flats hold bonefish, permit, barracuda, snook (around mangrove edges), sharks, and snappers. In northern latitudes, flats catches include redfish, stripers, bluefish, and sometimes seatrout.

FISHING BAYS
Bays can be large or small, with a mix of structure and fishing conditions as outlined above. When fishing a bay, don't be overwhelmed; simply treat each part of it as one of the above fishing situations, and fish accordingly.

Chapter 6

Popular Fly-Rod Species

The geographic ranges of fish vary, but different species with the same habitat requirements are often caught together or by using the same techniques. In tropical areas, expect to find bonefish, permit, barracuda, and sharks on the flats; snook and snappers around mangroves. In the mid-Atlantic, stripers are found with bluefish and sometimes seatrout or false albacore; flounder and sea bass are on the bottom in bays; shad, croaker, and white perch can be taken in season in both deep and shallow water. Along the northeast coast, look for stripers, bluefish, false albacore, mackerel, and tuna. On the northwest coast, you'll encounter shad, stripers, and salmon. In southwest coastal waters, expect to find Pacific barracuda and a host of inshore shallow- and deep-water species such as olive, blue, and copper rockfish; barred and spotted sand bass; corbina; whitefin and spotfin croaker; opaleye; and starry flounder. You'll also find tuna and pelagic species offshore. On the Gulf coast, you can expect seatrout, stripers, redfish, cobia, and sharks.

Fish can have teeth, crushers in their throats, sharp plates on the gills, or sharp spines in the fins or around the anal area and thus must be handled carefully. If you plan to eat your catch, ice the fish down immediately, make sure that melting ice water drains off, and check locally for possible dangers of fish poisoning. The most common of these is ciguatera, found in large Caribbean barracuda, as well as several hundred reef species. Ciguatera may cause death in severe cases. Older and larger fish are more likely to contain the toxin. Other poisons may be found in the skin, the liver of some sharks, the body organs of puffers, and the roe of certain species such as ladyfish and tarpon. Bacterial poisoning is also a possibility from scombroid fish, such as bluefish and tuna that are improperly preserved. With any species, botulism, staphylococcus, or streptococcus poisoning may result from poor preservation or cooking methods. Always use proper techniques for cleaning, preserving, and cooking your catch. Anglers are strongly advised to check more complete references before consuming fish.

Note: Seasons as listed below refer to when fish might be caught, not the legal seasons as defined by state or federal laws. Check before fishing.

AMBERJACK

Amberjack are basically southern deep-water fish, best caught with a fly rod by chumming them up from the bottom. Tough fish.

Size. Typically 10 to 30 pounds, but can exceed 100 pounds.

Location and Range. All along the southern Atlantic coast and south to Brazil, but mostly south of Cape Hatteras. They are inshore fish, often found over reefs and wrecks.

Seasons. They can be taken throughout the year, with the best fishing in spring through summer.

Habitat. Deep water, often around wrecks and reefs; smaller fish are found closer inshore.

Foods. Any baitfish, squid, flying fish.

Flies. Large streamers and poppers, chum flies, and Deceivers in sizes 1/0 to 5/0.

Tackle. Must be stout, since these are hard-fighting fish. Recommended are 12- to 15-weight outfits, with lifting power to keep the fish from diving into wrecks or coral. A heavy leader is also a must, as much for abrasion resistance as for strength.

Fishing Methods. Other than the occasional accidental catch, chumming is the best method, attracting the fish from the depths to the boat and then casting to them.

Special Considerations. Very tough fish; difficult to land. Handle with care, particularly if bringing large fish into the boat.

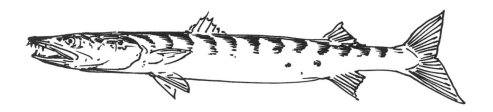

BARRACUDA

Size. Typically 10 to 20 pounds, but can exceed 75 pounds.

Location and Range. Both Atlantic and Pacific species are popular, found in tropical and subtropical areas of southern California, Florida, the Gulf of Mexico, and Central and South America.

Seasons. Caught year-round; best fishing spring through fall, since cool waters can send them deep or move them farther south.

Habitat. Often slowly cruising, while waiting to ambush prey. Often rest around structure, mangroves, along weed beds, and on break lines in channels. Found on flats when bonefishing, as well as cruising open water. Most large fish found singly, although smaller 'cudas school.

Foods. Eat nearly anything, but often needlefish and other slim, fast baitfish such as flying fish.

Flies. Long, slim needlefish imitations are often used, but other flies, such as Clousers and Deceivers, also work well. Can sometimes be taken on fast-moving skippers. Attracted to shiny objects, so some flash in a fly often helps. Best sizes are 1/0 to 4/0.

Tackle. Barracuda can grow big, so tackle must reflect the size of the fish expected. Best are 9- to 12-weight outfits, which are also necessary to cast the large flies used.

Fishing Methods. Usually sight fishing to a specific fish, casting well beyond it, and rapidly retrieving on a course to intercept it. Blind casting around known 'cuda spots such as piers, docks, pilings, and bridge supports is also ideal. In almost all cases, a fast two-handed retrieve is a must, especially when casting to barracuda spotted in open water. Always cast well beyond the barracuda and retrieve rapidly past the spot where the fish is expected. Use a wire bite leader. When retrieving, strip the line into a basket or other container, and clear the line immediately as the fish makes its first frantic run.

Special Considerations. Very sharp teeth—use extreme caution in handling and unhooking barracuda, both in and out of the water. They are also one of the main species known to cause ciguatera poisoning.

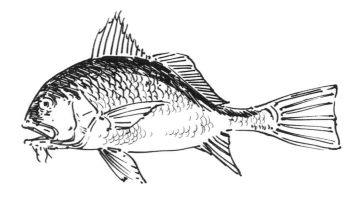

BLACK DRUM

Black drum are not as popular as red drum, more commonly called redfish. They are a poor food fish and are often too deep to be easily targeted by fly rodders.

Size. Typically 10 to 30 pounds but can exceed 100 pounds.

Location and Range. All along the Atlantic and Gulf coasts and south to Brazil.

Seasons. Best fishing from spring through summer, during migrations of the fish and when they are found in shallow water.

Habitat. Found in bays and estuaries on sandy, marl, and mud bottoms.

Foods. Eat almost any type of crustaceans or baitfish; crabs, clams, and oysters are favorites.

Flies. Any large sinking fly. If working over oyster areas that are prone to snags, use a bendback or keel hook style.

Tackle. They can get big, so tackle might be anything from a 10- to 15-weight outfit. Use short leaders with fast-sinking lines to get the fly down to the fish and keep it there during the retrieve.

Fishing Methods. Fish over areas known to hold black drum, perhaps chumming with crushed clams or crabs.

Special Considerations. Keep fingers out of the fish's mouth: Crushers in the back, used to crush oyster shells, can injure fingers.

BLUEFISH

Size. Typically 5 to 20 pounds, occasionally to 30 pounds.

Location and Range. Atlantic species found from mid–North Carolina to Cape Cod in the summer and wintering mostly offshore from the mid-Atlantic area south along the coast from Savannah, Georgia, to Miami. Spring through fall, they migrate into coastal areas and even tidal rivers, especially around the mid-Atlantic, which is also the prime nursery area.

Seasons. Midspring through midfall in most areas. They arrive as early as April in the Carolinas, as late as June in New England, and stay inshore through mid- to late fall.

Habitat. Constantly moving, free ranging, traveling in schools of the same-size fish, as larger blues would attack smaller ones. Feed heavily on all types of baitfish, particularly menhaden. Coastal in spring through fall, then winter offshore.

Foods. All types of baitfish, especially menhaden, a popular chum and bait. Slash their way through schools of bait, often leaving bits of bait and attracting gulls, which are a signal for breaking blues. Often birds will dive frantically over blues.

Flies. Depending on the fishing, skippers and poppers for breaking fish; Deceivers, Clousers, and other streamers for deep schools; chum flies when chumming in back of an anchored boat. Simple flies of synthetics are best, since the teeth of bluefish easily destroy flies and bugs.

Tackle. Baby blues can be taken on 8-weight or even smaller outfits, but the best fishing is with 9- or 10-weight outfits. Use a short, wire bite leader or special toothy critter flies tied to the bend, leaving a bare hook shank to serve as a short bite leader. Add a short wire leader on large fish.

Fishing Methods. Similar to stripers, with which they are occasionally mixed. Cast to breaking surface fish, blind-cast and fish deep if the depth finder shows fish in the area, or chum from an anchored boat. Because of the moving, schooling, and feeding nature of blues, most fly-rod catches are best when casting to breaking fish, or blind casting if schools are known to be in the area. Blues are not generally found around structure. Mostly boat fishing, but can be taken wading in shallow waters in the spring.

Special Considerations. Bluefish have sharp teeth, and many anglers agree that they seem to deliberately lunge at humans when caught. Use care in handling and unhooking, whether in the water or out. Must be iced immediately for food.

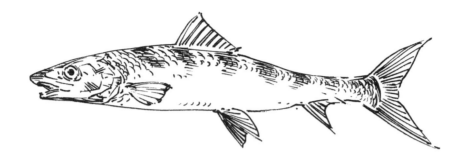

BONEFISH

Size. Typically 2 to 8 pounds, rarely to 15 pounds.

Location and Range. Worldwide in tropical and subtropical island and flats areas. Popular areas are southern Florida, Belize, Christmas Island, the Bahamas, and Las Roques, Venezuela. Must have 70-degree or warmer water.

Seasons. Fishing possible any time of year; best fishing spring through summer.

Habitat. Sand and turtle grass flats in tropical areas; sometimes found in cuts and channels when tides and dropping temperatures move the fish off the flats. Smaller fish feed in large schools on flats. As the fish become larger, they are found in smaller schools or singly.

Foods. Crabs, sea urchins, shrimp, sea worms, clams, and sometimes small fish found in feeding areas of flats, channels, and turtle grass. Feed mostly on the bottom, where they scrounge for food. On flats they can be found tailing, with their tails out of water as they root for food. Large schools often found in mud areas, sometimes with jack crevalle and stingrays.

Flies. Typical bonefish flies, MOE flies, crab and shrimp patterns. Most bonefish flies are point-up patterns with wings that cover and partly protect the point. Fished by hopping along the bottom in front of schools. Best hook sizes are 6 through 2.

Tackle. An 8-weight outfit is best, but you can go one or two sizes heavier or lighter if conditions and fish warrant.

Fishing Methods. Sight-fish flats by wading or boat fishing. Look for tailing bonefish, mudded areas of moving schools. Cast well ahead of the school, and move the fly in short hops only when the fish are on an intercepting or intersecting path. With a cold snap or low water on a high-tide flat, try blind casting for bones in channels adjacent to known feeding flats, perhaps even chumming for them with bits of shrimp or conch.

Special Considerations. Unhook rapidly and return to the water. To avoid stepping on stingrays, use a shuffling gait when wading flats to scare rays ahead of you.

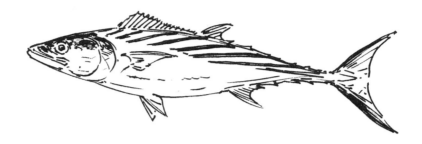

BONITO

In addition to the bonito described below, there is also a species found off eastern Australia, the only one with stripes on its belly.

Size. 3 to 8 pounds, occasionally to 15 pounds.

Location and Range. There is one Atlantic bonito, ranging from Nova Scotia to Argentina, and two eastern Pacific species, the Pacific bonito and the striped bonito. Bonito are pelagic, mostly staying well offshore, where they constantly migrate and feed.

Seasons. Best fishing in warm weather throughout the range.

Habitat. Oceangoing, schooling, pelagic, migratory species.

Foods. Follow schools of bait and will feed on almost any smaller oceangoing fish, baitfish, or squid.

Flies. Any large, baitlike patterns such as large Deceivers, streamers, or Whistlers. Large flies in sizes 1 to 3/0 tied with synthetics are best, providing bulk without weight.

Tackle. Most catches will be in the 5- to 10-pound range, and an 8-weight outfit will work fine but should include a reel with ample backing for long runs.

Fishing Methods. Bonito are often an occasional catch rather than a seriously targeted fly-rod species, but they can be caught by intercepting schools while trolling with conventional tackle.

Special Considerations. Strong fish for their size; make long runs.

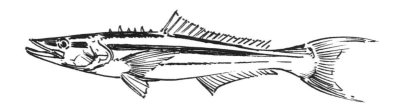

COBIA

Size. Typically 10 to 30 pounds, but can exceed 100 pounds.

Location and Range. Lower Chesapeake Bay and southward to Florida and the Gulf.

Seasons. Year-round in the southern parts of range; spring and fall in northern areas.

Habitat. Like structure. Often found around oil rigs, buoys, wrecks, reefs, bridge pilings, or anchored boats.

Foods. Eels, crabs, baitfish, squid, and shrimp.

Flies. Deceivers, crab patterns, eel flies, streamer flies, and poppers in sizes 1/0 through 5/0.

Tackle. Cobia can get big and are always tough. As a result, 10- to 12-weight outfits, and sometimes even larger, are best.

Fishing Methods. Blind-cast around typical open-water structure. Chumming also works to bring fish in close, where they can be reached easily with fly tackle.

Special Considerations. Cobia are very tough and never give up. Release carefully with the fish in the water or, if keeping, gaff and swing directly into the fish box, and immediately close the lid.

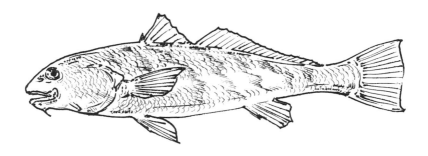

CORBINA

Size. Typically 1 to 4 pounds, occasionally to 8 pounds.

Location and Range. Inshore along the beach from the Gulf of California to Point Conception, California.

Seasons. Can be caught throughout the year, but fishing is best from summer through midfall.

Habitat. In the surf and tide line right up against the beach to about 40 feet deep along the shore. Favor a sandy surf environment.

Foods. About 90 percent of their diet is sand crabs or sand fleas, although they do eat other crustaceans and occasionally baitfish.

Flies. Flies that resemble sand crabs, sand fleas, or shrimp are best. Lacking specific patterns, any compact bulky fly, such as a Woolly Bugger or Whistler, in tan or brown colors that resemble a sand crab will work.

Tackle. These fish are small, with the largest recorded under 10 pounds, so any 8-weight outfit will handle them. Use moderately long leaders, as they are spooky and difficult to hook.

Fishing Methods. Cast into, and sometimes parallel to, the surf, working flies slowly and constantly. Strike as soon as any resistance is felt.

Special Considerations. Because of the way they chew and take in their food, they do not strike hard and are difficult to detect and hook. Use a slow, constant retrieve.

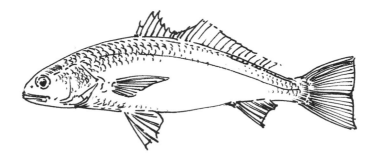

CROAKER

Size. 1 to 3 pounds.

Location and Range. Several croaker species are found throughout their range—croaker, or hardhead, and banded croaker from the Chesapeake Bay south through the Gulf, spotfin and yellowfin croaker off California south of Point Conception, and white croaker south of San Francisco.

Seasons. Best fishing is in the summer; the fish move deeper and offshore in winter, out of the reach of fly fishermen.

Habitat. Sandy bottoms, sometimes over oyster bars, in as shallow as a few feet of water, but often deeper.

Foods. Baitfish, crustaceans, crabs, and worms.

Flies. Any flies that imitate their foods; crab patterns, streamers, Clousers, Woolly Buggers, and worm patterns are ideal.

Tackle. Can be as light as a 6-weight, but often will have to be heavier to cast the weighted flies and sinking lines required.

Fishing Methods. Fish slowly and methodically over known croaker grounds using a full-sinking line, short leader, and weighted fly. Over oyster bars, use a weedless, bendback, or keel hook fly.

Special Considerations. Because croaker are small, they're not often targeted by fly fishermen. They make croaking sounds, hence the name.

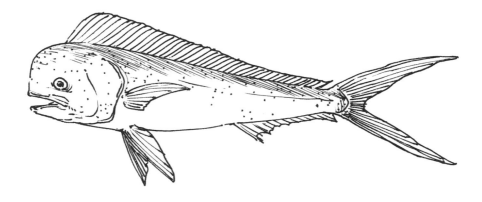

DOLPHIN

To avoid confusion with the mammal, this species is often referred to as dolphinfish. Also known as mahi mahi in the Pacific, and elsewhere as dorado.

Size. Typically 5 to 20 pounds, but 50-pounders have been taken on the fly rod and the fish can exceed 75 pounds.

Location and Range. Pelagic offshore species, found worldwide in warm, open seas.

Seasons. Because it is a fish of warm seas, best fishing is in spring through fall.

Habitat. Follow the Gulf Stream and other blue waters of the world. Often like to hide under floating weeds and debris—the best chance for fly rodders.

Foods. Baitfish of any type, but prefer flying fish.

Flies. Large streamers and poppers. Yellow or red and yellow is good in sizes 1/0 through 5/0, depending on fish size.

Tackle. Use 10-weight or heavier; up to 15-weight for big bull dolphin.

Fishing Methods. Cast to floating debris found while trolling; cast directly to fish if one is teased up to the boat transom.

Special Considerations. Dolphin will follow their hooked brethren, so for constant dolphin action by several fly rodders, keep a hooked fish in the water until a second is hooked.

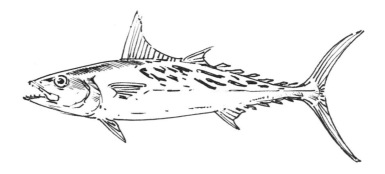

FALSE ALBACORE

Also known as albacore (though not the albacore that ends up in a tuna can) or little tunny.

Size. Typically 2 to 10 pounds, but sometimes to 20 pounds.

Location and Range. Found in warm waters of all oceans. Often found in northern latitudes such as Cape Cod but as far south as the Carolinas during fall migrations. Can come inshore around inlets while following bait, where they are most often targeted by fly fishermen, but more typically found offshore, sometimes breaking on the surface after bait.

Seasons. Best in summer through fall, when they migrate close inshore along the coast.

Habitat. Open waters; constantly swimming to take food.

Foods. Small baitfish, silversides, needlefish.

Flies. Small baitfish imitations, similar to Clousers, and tied with a prominent eye, in sizes 4 to 1.

Tackle. Best fishing with 8- to 9-weight outfit, with plenty of backing on the reel.

Fishing Methods. Find breaking schools (best in fall) and cast to them with small baitfish-imitation flies.

Special Considerations. Very fragile and must be released immediately by plunging them headfirst into the water or removing the fly from the fish while it is still in the water.

FLOUNDER AND FLUKE

Many species of flounder and the related fluke are found along all three coasts and are occasional fly-rod catches. Most are in the north Atlantic, where the summer flounder is popular; the starry flounder is popular in southern California.

Size. Usually 1 to 5 pounds, rarely to 15 pounds.

Location and Range. Found in both shallow and deep waters of all coasts. Most species are on the northern part of the coast, but some range as far south as Panama.

Seasons. Best in the summer, when they are shallow and more readily caught in shallow sloughs, fishing on a falling or low tide.

Habitat. Sandy bottoms, shallow sloughs between bars.

Foods. Minnows, silversides, sardines, shrimp, clams, other inshore bait.

Flies. Bendbacks, streamers, and keel hook patterns on long-shank hooks in sizes 6 to 1/0.

Tackle. Outfits from 8- to 10-weight, sinking or sinking-tip lines, short leaders, and minnow patterns tied on keel hooks or bendbacks. Short mono bite leader recommended.

Fishing Methods. Fish low or falling tides, casting into pockets and sloughs, allowing the line and fly to sink, and working the fly slowly along the bottom until the next cast.

Special Considerations. Difficult to land; use a net or small gaff if keeping for food.

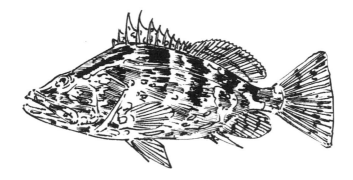

GROUPER

Grouper species include the Warsaw, red, black, and Nassau, as well as the related hinds, such as the rock, red, and speckled species and the jewfish. The hinds are basically small, but the jewfish can weigh far more than any fly rodder could ever handle. All are bottom species, some shallow and some deep water.

Size. Depends on the species, but usually 2 to 10 pounds, occasionally to 50 pounds.

Location and Range. Florida and other tropical and subtropical areas, including the Bahamas and Caribbean.

Seasons. Can be caught year-round.

Habitat. Coral, rocky areas, off bars and jetties, and sometimes around mangroves or Gulf coast oil rigs.

Foods. Other coral fish, baitfish, crustaceans, squid.

Flies. Any sinking or deep-water fly, particularly those with some bulk and body, such as Whistlers and Seaducers in sizes 2 through 5/0.

Tackle. Heavy tackle is a must, because these fish, once hooked, immediately turn and head for rocks or coral. They must be turned if you are to have a chance to land them. Use 12-weight or heavier tackle, with fast-sinking lines and long, heavy leaders to prevent your fly line from being abraded or cut when a fish heads into coral.

Fishing Methods. Chumming or fishing deep with meaty-looking flies works best, but these are difficult fish to specifically target. Otherwise, the best fishing is by working a fast-sinking line parallel to a sharp coral dropoff. When a fish strikes, immediately try to lever it away from the coral. You'll get more fish but will also have more break-offs than when working at right angles to the coral bank.

Special Considerations. Lifting power of the rod is the most important factor, along with heavy line and leaders to get the fish into open water.

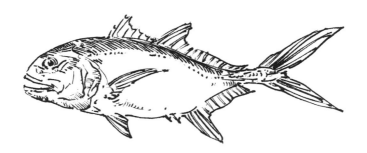

JACK CREVALLE

Jack crevalle are great when you catch the first one or two, but they are often scorned after that, when they can interfere with bonefish or tarpon catches. They are still a great, strong fish and in the right areas are easily taken on a fly.

Size. Typically 2 to 15 pounds, but fly-rod catches in the Atlantic have exceeded 40 pounds.

Location and Range. These are a common warm-water fish, with species in the Atlantic, Gulf of Mexico, Bahamas, and Caribbean, as well as the Pacific. They are commonly found in the same waters as permit, bonefish, tarpon, snappers, and other species.

Seasons. Warm water, spring through summer best.

Habitat. Jack are found almost anywhere—over reefs, sandy bottoms, marl, flats, channels, and around rockpiles and structure.

Foods. Schooling fish, jack will herd and feed on all manner of baitfish, including mullet, flying fish, menhaden, silversides, balao, and squid.

Flies. Large Deceivers, bonefish flies, needlefish patterns, eel patterns, streamers, Whistlers, and Clousers all work well in sizes 2 through 2/0.

Tackle. These are not huge fish, although they are strong. Best outfits are 8- to 12-weight, rigged with ample backing, a slow-sinking line, and a short leader.

Fishing Methods. Jack crevalle will crash and break on bait, at which time they can be fished by throwing a larger streamer or popper into the bait and retrieving rapidly. Other methods involve chumming in channels with bits of shrimp, just as for bonefish. They can also be found on flats, traveling in small schools or following mudding bonefish or rays.

Special Considerations. The flat sides of these fish allow them to constantly circle a boat when hooked, so use sideways pressure with the rod to turn the head of the fish as quickly as possible.

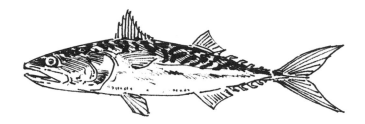

MACKEREL

Species include cero, king, narrow-barred, and Spanish mackerel.

Size. The cero and Spanish are similar and weigh about 5 to 10 pounds. The king and narrow-barred are often in the 20- to 30-pound range but can get considerably larger.

Location and Range. The Spanish, cero, and king mackerel are found in the Atlantic, often in temperate or warm waters or in the Tropics. The narrow-barred mackerel is found in the Pacific and Indian Oceans.

Seasons. Best in the summer, when the fish will follow warm ocean currents.

Habitat. Cero mackerel are often found near coral reefs, the other species mostly moving constantly and migrating in ocean currents.

Foods. Any baitfish, such as sardines, herring, anchovies, silversides, occasionally squid and shrimp.

Flies. Patterns that imitate locally favored baitfish, usually large flies such as Deceivers, Whistlers, and Clousers.

Tackle. Outfits should be 9- to 10-weight, larger for very large kings and narrow-barred. Use antireverse reels with ample backing of 30-pound-test Dacron, short leaders tipped with a short, single-strand wire bite leader.

Fishing Methods. Cast to teased fish; fish around reefs and structure for cero and narrow-barred mackerel; fish schools of bait or flying fish; fish around flotsam during dawn or dusk and during high or low, slack tides. Fish are often suspicious of a wire leader, but try a short length of single-strand wire.

Special Considerations. All mackerel have teeth—handle, land, and remove flies with care, and use tools.

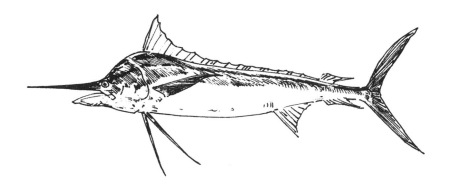

MARLIN

Size. Varies greatly among species. White marlin can reach 80 pounds, but a typical fly-rod size is 15 to 20 pounds. Blue marlin can reach 1,500 pounds, but the fly-rod record is just over 250 pounds.

Location and Range. Marlin are found worldwide, primarily in warm and tropical waters. Striped, blue, and black marlin occur in the Indian and Pacific Oceans, and white and blue marlin in the Atlantic.

Seasons. Primarily summer, but in tropical areas can be found migrating or following baitfish in the fall.

Habitat. Offshore in the open ocean, following warm currents and located around canyons. Follow baitfish such as mackerel, squid, and flying fish.

Foods. Squid, large baitfish such as mackerel, pilchards, anchovies, and flying fish.

Flies. Large flies, perhaps with a popper head, designed and tied to imitate locally favorite baits. Tube flies and popper heads also very popular and effective.

Tackle. Heavy tackle in the 13- to 17-weight range, rods designed for lifting and sight fishing, preferably antireverse reels with plenty of 30-pound-test backing capacity.

Fishing Methods. Tease fish to the stern of an offshore sportfisherman and cast to fish in the bait.

Special Considerations. Dangerous to handle and release; bill can be a formidable weapon. Handle with care.

PERMIT

The premier fly-rod fish.

Size. Typically 5 to 10 pounds, occasionally to 30 pounds, rarely to 40.

Location and Range. Tropical, found in the same waters as bonefish and tarpon.

Seasons. Spring through summer best.

Habitat. A wide fish that inhabits flats but requires deeper water than bonefish. Usually found singly rather than in schools.

Foods. Favors crustaceans; crabs are a favorite food.

Flies. Crab patterns best, followed by shrimp patterns, sizes 1 through 2/0.

Tackle. Outfits can range from 8- to 12-weight, since permit can go to 40 pounds or more. Plenty of backing a must. Use slow-sinking lines and long leaders.

Fishing Methods. Cast to spotted fish, allowing a crab fly to drift until picked up, or hop sinking crabs along the bottom.

Special Considerations. Very strong, powerful fish.

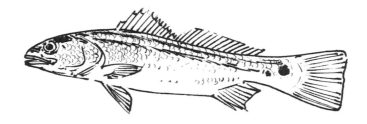

REDFISH

Also called red drum. Unlike black drum, redfish will migrate in shallow water, often with their backs almost out of the surface, making them easier prey for fly rodders.

Size. Typically 5 to 10 pounds, occasionally to 30 pounds.

Location and Range. The Atlantic coast from Maine to the Gulf of Mexico; most plentiful south of New Jersey.

Seasons. Mostly spring through fall, although in tropical and Gulf waters they can be caught year-round.

Habitat. Inshore sandy or muddy bottoms; around inlets, channels, and estuaries; in salt and brackish waters. Often found shallow and schooling in these waters, particularly during spring spawning seasons, and thus ideal fly-rod fish.

Foods. Baitfish, crabs, clams, mullet, worms, shrimp are all favored.

Flies. Patterns that imitate any of the above, with streamer flies preferred. Rattle flies are good, since mudding often occurs in shallows and the fish have poor eyesight.

Tackle. Use an 8- to 10-weight outfit, depending on size of fish targeted. Direct-drive or antireverse reels are fine, but be sure to have enough 20- or 30-pound backing. For some inshore fishing, when the fish are on the bottom, use a sinking-tip line and very short leader.

Fishing Methods. Cast to schooling or single fish; fish around inlets, channels, bays, and estuaries in favored areas. Virginia and North Carolina barrier islands and backcountry areas are excellent.

Special Considerations. Strong, tough fish. Rattle flies are easier for the fish to find.

ROCKFISH

The rockfish referred to here are west coast fish with over forty species and are not the striped bass called by this name in the Chesapeake Bay. About half the species are found in shallow water, including black, blue, olive, copper, and yellowtail, and half in deep water, including canary, vermillion, widow, green spotted, and starry.

Size. From 1 to 10 pounds, according to species. The vermillion can reach 15 pounds.

Location and Range. Various species are found from Mexico to Alaska in inshore waters, deep or shallow.

Seasons. Best fishing in summer.

Habitat. Often over rocky areas or reefs. Most are difficult targeted fly-rod catches, but some, such as the yellowtail and olive rockfish, are often close to the surface, where they are taken on streamer flies.

Foods. Baitfish, squid, octopus, shrimp, sardines, anchovies, crabs, depending on the species.

Flies. Best starter flies are small streamers, sizes 6 to 1, in white, yellow, black, and chartreuse, since most of these fish are not that large.

Tackle. An 8-weight rig with fast- and full-sinking line, short leader, and weighted streamer fly works best, for all are small fish. Use a slow-sinking line if the fish are near the surface.

Fishing Methods. Cast and count down to get the fly to the fish, then retrieve slowly. Because fishing is over a rocky bottom, bendback, keel, or weedless flies are best.

ROOSTERFISH

The roosterfish is named for the high dorsal spines that become erect when it is excited.

Size. Typically 5 to 20 pounds, but can exceed 100 pounds.

Location and Range. Found from the Gulf of California to Peru.

Seasons. Mostly summer, but good catches also taken in winter.

Habitat. An inshore species sometimes found in the surf as well as over sandy bottoms in moderate depths.

Foods. Any small fish and ocean baitfish.

Flies. Any large fly that can be cast that resembles local baitfish or prey.

Tackle. Can be large, so 10- to 12-weight or larger outfits best, using an antireverse reel with plenty of backing.

Fishing Methods. Cast to the fish, blind-cast along the shore when they are plentiful there, or tease fish to the boat while trolling, then cast.

Special Considerations. The fish jump a lot and may throw the hook. A tough fish.

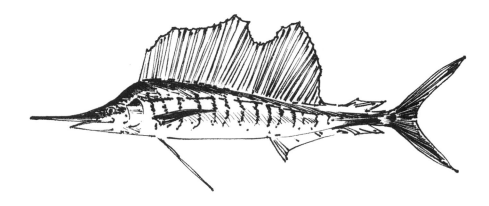

SAILFISH

Size. Typical fly-rod catch is between 10 and 50 pounds, occasionally to 100 pounds. Pacific sailfish are generally larger than Atlantic, and can reach 200 pounds.

Location and Range. A tropical and subtropical species, following warm ocean currents, along with marlin and wahoo. Caught in both the Atlantic and Pacific.

Seasons. Warm-water seasons best, but in tropical areas, this can be almost any time of the year.

Habitat. Ocean, migratory, pelagic, following schools of bait and food.

Foods. Bait, small fish, squid, mackerel, tuna, jack, ballyhoo, needlefish, flying fish, mullet.

Flies. Any large fly that simulates any of the above natural foods.

Tackle. Use a 12-weight outfit or larger, even though the fish tires easily and rapidly. Reels should be antireverse with large backing capacity.

Fishing Methods. Tease to a trolling offshore sportfisherman, then cast to the teased fish from a dead boat.

Special Considerations. Handle and release carefully; watch out for the bill.

SAND BASS

Size. 1 to 5 pounds.

Location and Range. Monterey, California, and south for spotted sand bass; Santa Cruz, California, and south for barred sand bass.

Seasons. Best spring through fall, with peak seasons in early summer.

Habitat. Barred on sandy bottoms; spotted around underwater structure. Can be shallow but are often deep—sometimes too deep for fly fishing.

Foods. Crustaceans, octopus, squid, baitfish.

Flies. Small streamer flies that imitate baitfish, squid, or crustaceans.

Tackle. Full- and fast-sinking lines a must, with short leaders on 8-weight outfits.

Fishing Methods. Chum using live baitfish to bring fish to the boat, or cast when a school is located on the depth finder, then use the count-down method to get the fly to the fish.

Special Considerations. Chumming is most effective for fly fishing, but it takes time for fish to gather at the boat.

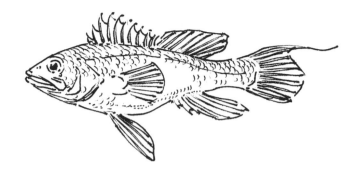

SEA BASS

The large family of sea bass also includes the grouper and hinds. The sea bass of the Atlantic is a small, inshore species easily caught on flies.

Size. Typically 1 to 4 pounds, occasionally to 7 pounds.

Location and Range. From Maine to Florida and the eastern half of the Gulf of Mexico.

Seasons. Best fishing in late spring through early fall.

Habitat. In bays and inshore over the continental shelf, around jetties, pilings, structure, wrecks, and rocks. Can be shallow or deep.

Foods. Baitfish and some crustaceans.

Flies. Any small streamer fly, sizes 4 to 1/0. Since these are bottom fish, bendbacks or keel flies are best.

Tackle. Full-sinking lines with short leader best, on 7- or 8-weight outfit.

Fishing Methods. Cast around inshore structure such as rocks, pilings, jetties, wrecks, and rocks.

Special Considerations. Often caught incidentally when targeting other inshore species on the Atlantic coast.

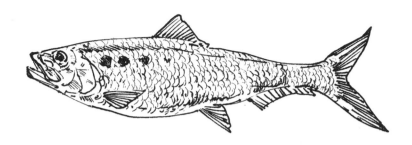

SHAD

There are two species, the white, or American, and the hickory shad. Both are found all along the Atlantic, but it is not known how plentiful and widespread the hickory is. White shad have been introduced to the northern Pacific coast.

Size. White shad average 1 to 3 pounds, occasionally to 7 pounds. The hickory averages smaller.

Location and Range. From the St. Johns River in Florida to Newfoundland on the Atlantic coast, and all along the Pacific coast to Alaska. Mostly offshore, but come inshore to ascend rivers to spawn each spring.

Seasons. The best fishing is in the spring, but the season ranges from January or February in the south to late June in the north.

Habitat. Ascends natal streams and rivers to spawn.

Foods. Unknown whether it eats in natal rivers, but it is now thought to. It does hit, although this might be reflexive.

Flies. Small, colorful flies, without excessive shiny materials such as mylar, and in small sizes on regular-shank, size 8 through 4 hooks.

Tackle. Outfits in the 7- to 9-weight range, with ample backing. Sinking or sinking-tip lines fished with short leaders are suggested to get the fly down to the fish and keep it down.

Fishing Methods. Cast cross-stream or cross-current in estuary areas, allowing the fly to swing with the current where it is bumped by the fish.

Special Considerations. Shooting tapers allow greater casting distances for more thorough fishing and are most popular on the west coast.

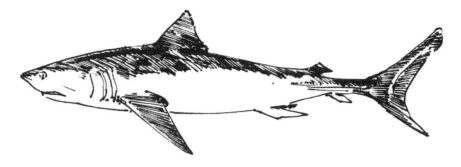

SHARKS

There are several hundred species of sharks, and many can be sought and caught by the fly angler. Inshore species, such as blacktip, lemon, sand, dusky, and brown, are common in shallow waters and are taken when they are on flats (southern species) or by chumming. Offshore species, such as mako, tiger, blue, and hammerhead, come inshore to feed and some to spawn.

Size. Varies greatly according to species and location. Hammerheads and makos in the 10- to 100-pound range are taken by fly fishers in the Florida Keys.

Location and Range. Worldwide, with common fly-rod catches including the blue, hammerhead, mako, porbeagle, thresher, tiger, and white. Some are most common to specific areas of coast, such as the brown, found primarily in the mid-Atlantic; the dusky, in the north Atlantic; the lemon and blacktip, in tropical waters; and the bonnet shark, on the Pacific coast and southern Atlantic.

Seasons. Year-round, although most are more prevalent in fishing areas from spring through fall.

Habitat. Sharks are open-ocean fish, although they come inshore to feed and spawn, and some travel up coastal rivers. In the Tropics, such as Florida and the Bahamas, lemon and blacktip sharks are commonly sought on shallow flats.

Foods. Most sharks are flesh eaters and opportunistic feeders. They favor fresh food, so any chum should be fresh. Depending on the species, they will eat any other fish, other sharks, sometimes lobsters and crabs, and larger baitfish.

Flies. Large flies and poppers are best, cast close to the fish and immediately worked, because most sharks have poor eyesight. Rattle flies are also good. Chum flies are ideal when chumming. Sizes of flies can range from 2 through 6/0.

Tackle. Depending on the size of the shark, you may need anything from an 8- or 9-weight outfit to as heavy as a 15- to 17-weight rig. Intermediate lines are usually better than floating to maintain contact with the fly. A short leader with a wire bite tippet is a must.

Fishing Methods. Sight-fish on flats or chum in open water from a drifting or anchored boat, then cast to individual fish if possible. Some sharks will follow trolled baits and can be teased to the boat and cast to using marlin techniques.

Special Considerations. All sharks have teeth and must be considered extremely dangerous. If releasing and the fly can't be removed, cut the leader using a long-handled dehooker. If keeping, use a gaff only and tie off the fish by the tail, but don't bring it into the boat even if it appears to be dead.

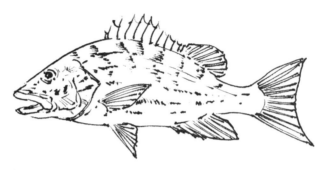

SNAPPERS

The seventeen species of snappers in North America are found mostly around reefs and rocks, from the shallows to very deep. Many, but not all, are tropical.

Size. Most species average between 2 and 10 pounds. Pacific cubera snappers over 30 pounds have been caught on the fly.

Location and Range. Many species are found from Florida south, and others all along the Atlantic and Pacific coasts.

Seasons. In southern warm waters, fishing possible year-round, but shallow-water and flats fishing best spring through fall.

Habitat. Commonly found around rocks, reefs, mangroves, and channels, but mutton snappers are also found on flats, where they sometimes tail like bonefish.

Foods. All species have teeth, and most feed on baitfish.

Flies. MOE patterns, bonefish flies on flats, small streamers, Deceivers, Whistlers, and Clousers.

Tackle. Some, such as the mutton snapper, can go to 25 pounds or more, and tackle must reflect expected fish—mostly from an 8- to a 10-weight outfit. Floating lines OK if the fish are shallow or on flats, but slow- or medium-sinking lines best for most fishing.

Fishing Methods. Blind-cast around mangroves, over reefs, rocks, and in channels. Sight-fish with MOE or bonefish flies on flats.

Special Considerations. Snappers have lots of teeth; use a heavy mono bite tippet.

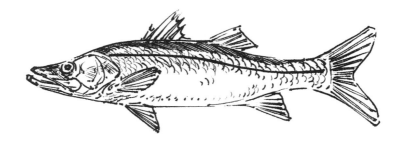

SNOOK

Snook are similar to largemouth bass in habitat, foods, and fishing methods and are often a favorite for freshwater anglers in the Tropics and those who are new to saltwater fishing. There are six species each in the Atlantic and Pacific.

Size. Typically 3 to 15 pounds, with fly-rod trophies to 30 pounds.

Location and Range. Snook are found in the Tropics and seldom survive in water below 60 degrees F. Found mostly in shallow water, in saltwater shallows, flats, and bars and in brackish water, and sometimes in freshwater rivers and estuaries, depending on season.

Seasons. Can be caught year-round, but best fishing is April through early September. June and July good for big fish.

Habitat. Commonly found around mangroves, docks, bridge pilings, bulkheads, mud banks, and similar structure.

Foods. Will eat a wide variety of crustaceans, such as shrimp, crabs, and small saltwater crayfish, along with any small fish or baitfish.

Flies. Flies that imitate pinfish, crabs, shrimp, mullet, and similar baitfish, along with poppers and sliders, are ideal snook flies in sizes 1 through 3/0.

Tackle. They get bigger than bass, so anything from an 8- to 10-weight outfit is best. Use the heavy tackle along with heavier leaders to turn fish if fishing around mangroves. Floating or slow-sinking lines are best in daytime fishing, fast-sinking lines and short leaders when fishing around bridge pilings at night.

Fishing Methods. Look for the saltwater equivalent of bass structure—mangroves, trees, and branches along the shore, docks, bridge pilings, bulkheads, coves, bars, and the like. Cast as close as possible into such structure, and favor shady sides of structure during the day, as snook won't be back in the structure or mangroves as far under the shady conditions.

Special Considerations. Snook are hard fighters. They are pretty fish with a pronounced lateral line, but they have a razor-sharp plate on the back of the gills—be careful, and if landing by the gill plate, keep your hand well forward and under the gills and in the mouth.

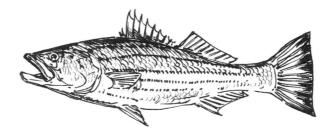

STRIPED BASS

Striped bass, called rockfish in the mid-Atlantic, are a popular and easily caught fly-rod fish.

Size. Fish can range from pan-size up to 70 pounds or more, although most caught on flies will be smaller than 25 pounds.

Location and Range. Throughout the Atlantic coast to northern Florida, and transplanted from Washington State to northern California. Mostly inshore and coastal, traveling into brackish and fresh waters to spawn. The Hudson River, Delaware River, Chesapeake Bay, and San Francisco Bay are hot spots.

Seasons. Year-round; best in spring and fall, when they are more actively feeding.

Habitat. Coastal, in bays, inlets, over oyster bars, and around river inlets. Prevalent around structure, including man-made features, such as bridges, pilings, breakwaters, and jetties. They ascend tidal rivers in the spring to spawn. Often travel in schools by size, and by sex when spawning.

Foods. Voracious predator. Will eat smelt, spearing, silversides, eels, killifish, sand eels, menhaden, crabs, and shrimp.

Flies. Large streamers, Blondes, Deceivers, Whistlers, Seaducers, Clousers, shrimp patterns, eel patterns, popping bugs, and skippers. Best colors are white, black, and yellow.

Tackle. Use an 8- to 10-weight, with 100 or more yards of backing.

Fishing Methods. Blind-cast to structure, especially during a moving tide, by casting upcurrent of structure and working or drifting the flies through the area, keeping a snug line to detect strikes. Also cast poppers, sliders, or flies to breaking fish. An ideal method to take bigger fish is to cast a weighted fly on a sinking line to get underneath the often-smaller breaking fish. A good way to attract fish to the boat is to tease them with a cast, hookless plug. Also good is casting to sighted spawning fish during the spring. Chumming is ideal, fishing from an anchored boat in shallow water or over shoals, with fleshy-looking chum flies on a short leader and sinking-tip line, drifting the fly in the chum close to the boat transom.

Special Considerations. Often the larger fish are deep, requiring a fast-sinking line or sinking shooting taper, short leader, and weighted fly to reach them. Can be slow fishing but productive on big stripers. Structure-strewn shallows are also ideal, working popping bugs fast. Be ready for explosive strikes—sometimes the fish will miss the bug. Continue the same retrieve until getting a solid hookup.

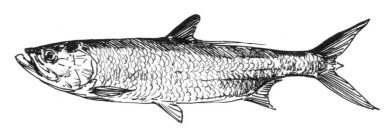

TARPON

One of the premier fly-rod game fish. The tarpon has a primitive lung system, or air bladder, that allows it to take in air by gulping and thus live for a time in stagnant areas or fresh water.

Size. Typically 5 to 50 pounds, but specimens over 180 pounds have been caught on the fly.

Location and Range. Found in the Atlantic in tropical and warm temperate areas, occasionally as far north as lower Virginia.

Seasons. Taken year-round, but top seasons vary with the locale. Shallow fly-rod fish caught mostly from March through July. On the west coast of Florida, March through June is best for big tarpon.

Habitat. Tarpon can be found inshore or offshore, on flats, in channels, and sometimes in deep water, although fly rodders seek them mostly by sight fishing on flats or in channels. They have specific migration patterns based on season and water temperature, so their movements can be predicted.

Foods. Pinfish, mullet, shrimp, crabs, and other baitfish.

Flies. Flies can include any baitfishlike streamer or crustacean pattern, such as shrimp and crab flies. Most flies are the sparse Stu Apte style for fishing flats or the bushier Whistler style for pushing water and fishing deep. Best sizes are 1 through 4/0.

Tackle. Because tarpon vary so widely in size, tackle can range from about 7- to 12-weight. Best lines are slow-sinking clear lines, to avoid scaring the fish, along with standard leaders and tough tippets.

Fishing Methods. Fly fishing for tarpon usually involves sight fishing from a boat, casting to intercept fish cruising on a flat or migrating in a channel. Fly position and sink rate are critical to place the fly in the right position in front of or alongside the tarpon.

Special Considerations. Tarpon are not eaten, so all should be released. These fish have very tough, bony mouths, so extremely sharp hooks are a must.

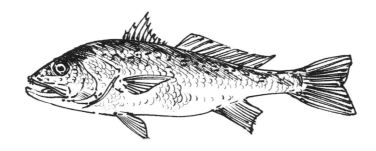

WEAKFISH AND SEATROUT

The silver seatrout, spotted seatrout, and weakfish are related species that occur along the Atlantic coast and in the Gulf.

Size. The silver seatrout grows to 14 inches; the spotted seatrout, to 28 inches; and the weakfish, to 35 inches.

Location and Range. The spotted seatrout and weakfish overlap in range from New England to Florida, with the spotted seatrout also prevalent in the Gulf of Mexico. The weakfish is caught mostly from New England to Virginia, the spotted seatrout mostly along the southern states and in the Gulf, and the silver seatrout only south of the Chesapeake Bay.

Seasons. Best fishing from midspring through fall, with longer seasons the farther south you go.

Habitat. Over sandy areas, around structure and mud banks, and in salt marshes. Larger fish are solitary except during the spring spawning. The silver seatrout is a deep-water fish except in winter.

Foods. Baitfish mostly, along with squid and some crustaceans.

Flies. Streamers, Clousers, Blondes, Deceivers, and other baitfish imitations, along with shrimp and squid patterns in sizes 1 through 3/0.

Tackle. Ideal outfit is an 8- to 9-weight rig, casting sinking-tip or full-sinking lines, depending on the depth of the fish. Intermediate or slow-sinking lines OK around mud banks and salt marshes.

Fishing Methods. Cast to schooled fish found on depth finder in spawning season, or chum area and blind-cast small streamers.

Special Considerations. Can be overfished in schools; release if not keeping a few for food.

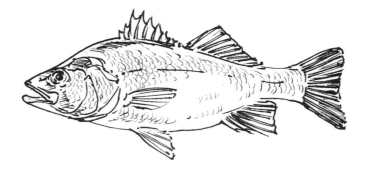

WHITE PERCH

White perch are easy fish to catch. They are also found in fresh water, mostly in the northern part of their range, and thus they are one with which freshwater fly rodders might be familiar.

Size. Typically less than a pound, rarely to 3 pounds.

Location and Range. Salt marshes, bays, and inshore brackish waters from New England through St. Johns River, Florida. Very abundant in the Hudson River and Chesapeake Bay.

Seasons. Can be caught year-round; best fishing from midspring through fall.

Habitat. Found in variety of habitats—on sandy bottoms, over oyster bars, and around rocks, wrecks, and other structure.

Foods. Small baitfish, but will also eat worms, crustaceans, grass shrimp, and other prevalent bait.

Flies. Small, bright flies similar to steelhead or shad flies are best, in sizes 8 to 2.

Tackle. Can be as light as you like if you can throw the flies; a 6- to 7-weight outfit usually best.

Fishing Methods. Cast to chummed or schooling species spotted on depth finder. Can be deep, requiring a full-sinking line, or shallow, where a slow-sinking line is adequate.

Special Considerations. These are small panfish but they're plentiful and fun to catch.

Chapter 7

Tying Basic Saltwater Patterns

There are good reasons for tying your own flies and bugs. Tying your own will save money (though not as much as you might expect); it is a fun hobby, especially in the winter when you can't fish; and you can make or customize exactly what you wish to try and develop new patterns.

TOOLS
You will need several tools, none of which need be expensive. They include the following:

• **Vise.** A good fly-tying vise is a must. Many good, inexpensive models are available. Choose between the clamp style, which clamps to the edge of a table, and the pedestal style, which has a heavy base and rests on a table. Make sure that the vise has jaws to hold hooks in the saltwater range—about size 6 through 5/0.

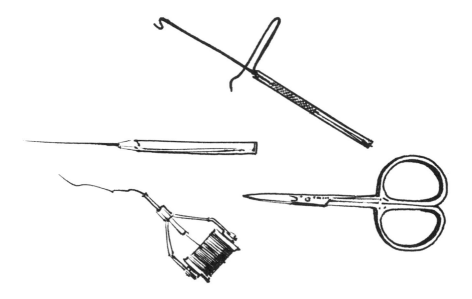

• **Scissors.** You need two pairs of scissors—one coarse pair with serrated blades, for rough cutting of tough materials such as synthetics, and a small pair with short, fine, sharp points. Buy fly-tying scissors, not sewing scissors, to get the larger finger holes that most tiers require.

• **Bobbins.** Bobbins hold thread to allow easy wrapping and make tying easier. Best are those with ceramic tips to prevent grooving the tube or cutting the thread.

• **Bodkin.** A bodkin is nothing more than a sharp needle held in a handle. You can make one from a short length of wood dowel and a long sewing needle. Use a bodkin for depositing head cement on flies, picking out fur bodies, and similar tasks.

• **Whip Finisher.** Whip finishes to secure the thread can be done by hand, but a whip-finisher tool allows for easy finishing of the fly head.

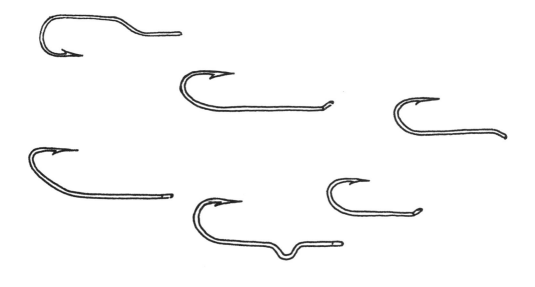

HOOKS

Hooks vary widely. Sizes for saltwater flies range from size 6 (small) through size 5/0 (large). Many finishes, styles, hook bends, hook points, and eye types are available. Most for salt water are regular or long-shank, made of stainless steel or with a protective finish to prevent corrosion. Some specialty hooks include keel hooks, bendback hooks, long-shank kink-shank hooks for poppers and sliders, and very stout ocean hooks for big game fly fishing. Sharpen hooks and make any other modifications before tying (see chapter 2). That way, if the hook breaks, it will be before you've invested time and materials in tying a fly.

WEEDLESS HOOKS

Many saltwater fish like weeds. Weedless flies and bugs make it possible to fish these spots. There are several simple possibilities.

Continuous Mono Weedguard. Before starting to tie a fly, tie in one or two lengths of 20- to 30-pound mono at the upper part of the hook bend. Then tie the fly. Before wrapping off and finishing the head, pull the mono forward and tie off as well, making sure that the mono loop extends slightly outside the hook point. Trim.

Wire Weedguard. Light wire (about 0.012) can be folded in half, the folded ends bent at a point where the fold will catch the hook point, then tied into place before finishing a fly head.

Single and Double Mono Weedguards. Twenty- to 30-pound mono can be folded into a sharp bend, the short end tied into a fly head, and the long end clipped where it will extend down and protect the hook point. Doubled mono can be used the same way. The same can be done with bugs, or you can punch holes into the bug belly on either side of the hook shank, glue mono into the holes, and clip the mono to length.

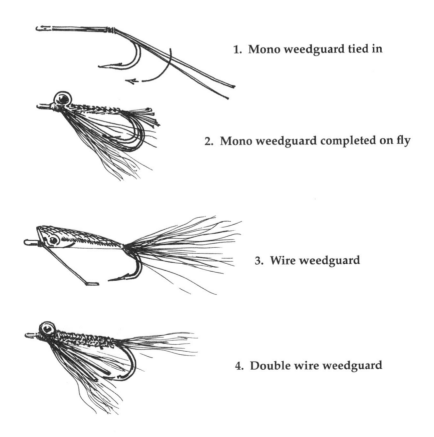

1. Mono weedguard tied in

2. Mono weedguard completed on fly

3. Wire weedguard

4. Double wire weedguard

BASICS OF TYING, WRAPS, AND FINISHING

The basics of tying are to wrap around the hook with the thread several times, then cross over these wraps several more times to secure. This tie-on can be at any point on the hook, depending on how you plan to tie it. It is often best at the head of the fly.

Secure body materials the same way, by wrapping the thread over an end of the material, then wrapping the material along the hook shank. Tie down wing and tail materials by holding the wing or tail on top of the hook shank, bringing the thread straight up and lightly over the wing, then straight down on the opposite side. This prevents the material from cocking to one side.

To finish a fly, use a whip finish, which is a wrap of thread around the head of the fly and the standing thread at the same time—the same technique used to whip the end of a rope. This can be done by hand or with a whip finisher.

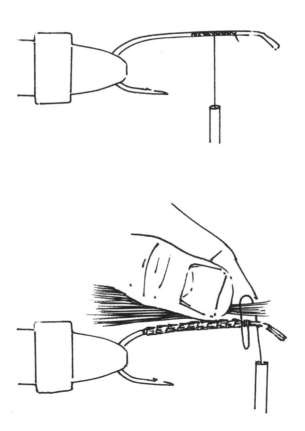

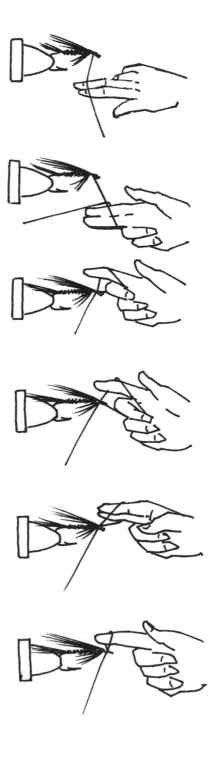

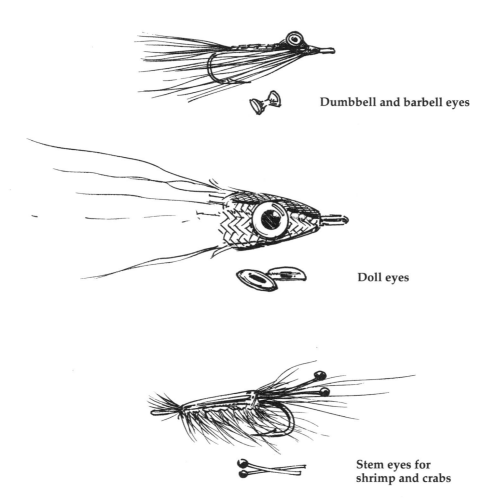

Dumbbell and barbell eyes

Doll eyes

Stem eyes for shrimp and crabs

EYES ON FLIES

Most fly fishermen and fly tiers agree that predators, especially saltwater fish, target eyes in prey species. Eyes can be added to any pattern, using glue-on or stick-on prism eyes, doll eyes, plastic eyes, wrapped stem eyes of mono for shrimp and crab patterns, tied-on eyes such as bead chain or lead dumbbell, or painted eyes. Glue-on, stick-on, and painted eyes are best protected by coating the eyes and head with epoxy. Make stem eyes by burning 50- to 100-pound-test mono to make round, black balls, then tying the stems to the hook shank.

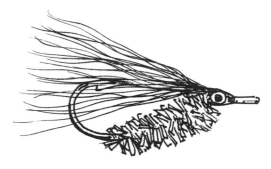

2. **Cover with body material.**

1. **Tie in rattle.**

Rattle Flies

Some saltwater fish have very poor eyesight or are fished for in muddy water. Both situations make it visually difficult for a fish to locate a fly. To compensate, some tiers make flies with plastic, glass, or aluminum worm rattles tied to the hook shank and then covered with body material. To work, they must be twitched frequently.

Tying Flies

Unlike most freshwater flies, saltwater flies are difficult to pigeonhole. They encompass a wide variety of tying styles and techniques to imitate a wide variety of natural saltwater forage. The following are some basics for any saltwater fly box. Suggested hook sizes are based on the fly's probable usage, but any fly can be tied smaller or larger.

DECEIVERS

Developed by Lefty Kreh, this fly is a basic design that is highly suggestive of a number of minnows. It will not foul on the cast and is easy to tie. It can be tied in many different colors, with or without toppings and with or without flash material in the wings. It is probably the most popular style of saltwater fly. It can be made on small or huge hooks, dressed sparsely or full, as desired. Suggested hook sizes: 4 through 3/0.

Step 1. Tie in the thread at the bend of the hook, and tie on three pairs of white saddle hackles (use more or less, depending upon hook size and fly style). Tie in flat to simulate a baitfish, flared for more action or to imitate a squid.

Step 2. Tie in mylar silver tinsel or similar tinsel body material.

Step 3. Wrap thread forward, followed by evenly wrapped tinsel.

Step 4. Tie off tinsel and clip excess, then tie in white calf tail or bucktail. Position this collar to surround the hook shank.

Step 5. Clip excess fur and wrap head.

Step 6. Whip-finish head and seal with epoxy or head cement.

Variations: Can be tied in any color or tied with a topping of peacock herl to simulate the dark back of a baitfish.

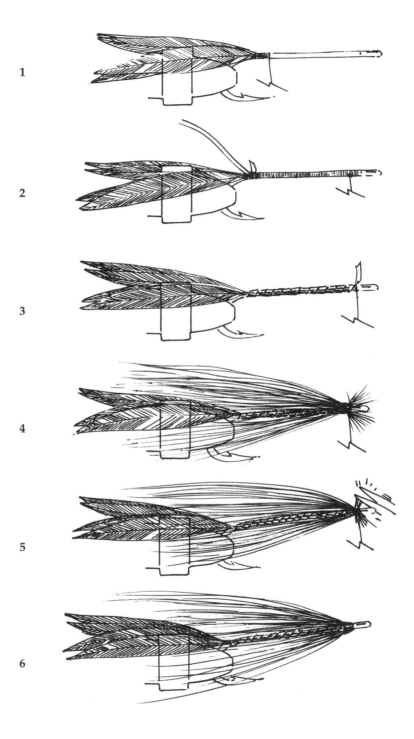

TARPON FLIES

Tarpon flies can be bulky or sparse, but a typical one for Florida Keys fishing in clear, shallow water is tied completely at the rear of the hook shank and features a bare or painted hook shank. A fuller style, more like a Whistler or Seaducer, is better for deep or murky water, since it pushes water to allow fish to find the fly. This is a Florida Keys style as used by Stu Apte. Suggested hook sizes: 1 to 4/0, depending on tarpon size.

Step 1. Tie in bright orange thread at the rear of the hook shank.

Step 2. Tie in multiple pairs of bright orange and bright yellow saddle hackles for the wing. Secure and clip excess hackle.

Step 3. Tie in bright orange and bright yellow hackle to palmer as the collar.

Step 4. Wind hackle around the area at the rear of the hook shank. Wrap forward slightly and tie off. Wrap thread forward and back on the hook shank, flaring the hackle slightly back as you do so, and building up a tapered long head on the hook shank.

Step 5. Finish up at the hackle, and tie off with a whip finish.

Step 6. Seal the long head with clear head cement or epoxy.

Variations: Color combinations of black, tan, red, and brown can be tied in the same style. Deep-water flies to push water can be started the same way but completed like a Whistler or Seaducer, covering the hook shank with lead fuse wire and finishing with a longer, bulkier wrap of hackle that covers the hook shank.

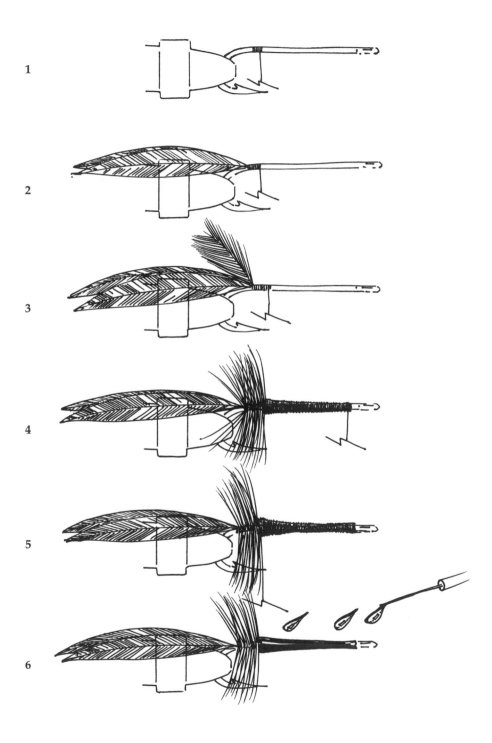

WHISTLERS AND SEADUCERS

Homer Rhode developed the Seaducer, and Dan Blanton created the Whistler. They are similar flies. The Whistler is one of the best deep-water flies, with its wrap of lead wire and bead chain eyes to give the fly a rapid sink rate. The Seaducer has a full wrap of hackle in front of what is usually a saddle hackle tail and no fuse wire or chenille wrap. The following is for a basic Whistler. Suggested hook sizes: 1 to 4/0.

Step 1. Tie in thread in back of hook eye, and tie in a pair of bead chain eyes, figure-eighting them in place. Wrap thread to rear of hook shank.

Step 2. Tie in a bundle of bucktail, and clip excess bucktail forward of wrap.

Step 3. Tie down a length of lead fuse wire, and make several wraps of the wire around the hook shank. Clip excess and tie off.

Step 4. Tie in a length of chenille over the bucktail wrap, and wrap thread to the middle of the hook shank. Take two or three turns of chenille around the hook, and tie off with thread, clipping the excess chenille.

Step 5. Tie in several hackles at this point, and wrap the thread forward to just in back of the bead chain eyes. Palmer the hackle forward to make a dense hackle collar, tying off at the bead chain eyes.

Step 6. Clip excess hackle, finish the head of the fly, and tie off with a whip finish. Seal with head cement or epoxy.

Variations: Use any color combination of bucktail and hackle. On some styles, grizzly hackle is used over the wing to make a barred pattern.

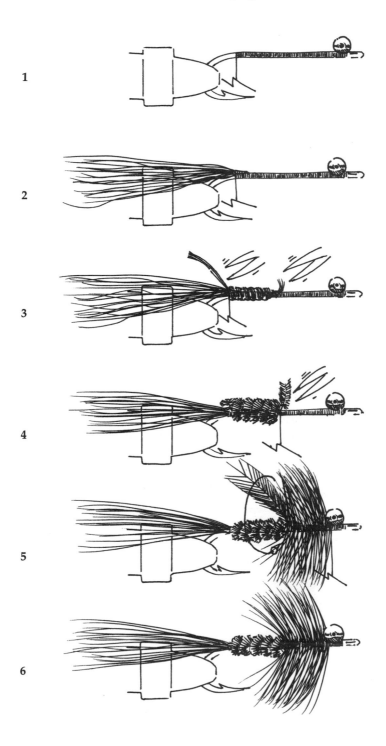

BONEFISH OR PERMIT FLIES

There are hundreds of patterns of bonefish flies; many bonefish books include patterns, and one book is devoted exclusively to the subject. Materials and colors vary widely. Most are tied to ride point-up with the wing covering the hook point.

The following is a generic-style basic bonefish fly, which can be modified in tail, body, and wing as desired, provided that it rides and looks as above. Suggested hook sizes: 6 to 1/0, with size 4 the best for most bonefish.

Step 1. With the hook in the vise point-down, tie in the thread at the head of the fly, then tie in a pair of bead chain eyes, figure-eighted with thread around the hook shank.

Step 2. Wrap to the rear of the hook shank, and tie in a strand of chenille. Wrap the thread forward.

Step 3. Wrap the chenille forward and tie off in back of the bead chain eyes. Clip the excess chenille.

Step 4. Turn the hook over so that it's in the vise point-up, and tie down a bundle of calf tail or bucktail. The end of this wing should cover the point of the hook.

Step 5. Clip the excess wing material forward of the wrap. Compete the head by wrapping around the eyes, and finish wrapping the wing.

Step 6. Tie off with a whip finish, and seal with head cement or epoxy.

Variations: Floss or yarn can be used for the body, overwrapped with clear monofilament. You can also vary the wing materials, adding hackle or using hackle alone, and you can use lead or plastic doll eyes in place of the bead chain. Clousers and other small, simple flies also work well for bonefish and permit, and crab flies are excellent for permit.

1

2

3

4

5

6

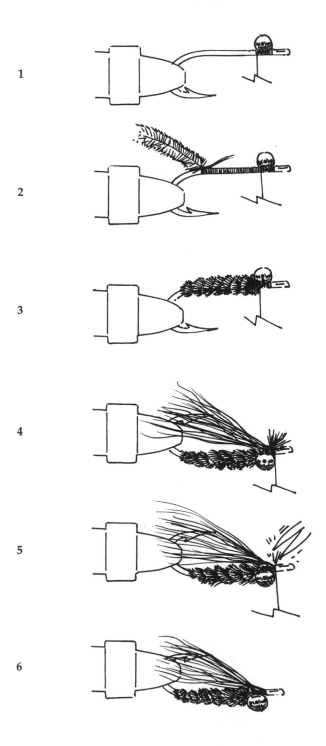

MOTHER OF EPOXY (MOE) FLIES

Mother of epoxy (MOE) flies are made with epoxy bodies that are usually diamond shaped. They settle on the bottom nicely, ride point-up, are durable, and catch fish. The following is for a basic MOE. Suggested hook sizes: 6 to 1.

Step 1. Insert a regular-shank-length hook point-up into the vise, and tie on the thread at the bend of the hook.

Step 2. Tie in flared wing material such as hackle feathers, stranded synthetics, bucktail, or calf tail. Clip excess material, wrap the thread forward, and tie off in back of the hook eye.

Step 3. Cut a small diamond shape of colored, translucent vinyl or acetate, and glue to the hook shank. Use cyanoacrylate glue (superglue).

Step 4. Glue colored plastic beads to the tips of the diamond shape.

Step 5. Mix five-minute clear epoxy, and spread carefully on the top and bottom of the diamond-shaped form, sealing the thread wrap and eyes.

Step 6. Rotate on a fly rotator for several minutes until cured. Ideally, the epoxy will be flattened and evenly spread over the diamond-shaped form, which will give the MOE fly its color.

Variations: Lead split shot can be used in place of colored beads for a faster-sinking fly. Hooks with MOE blanks are available that require only tying in the tail to complete.

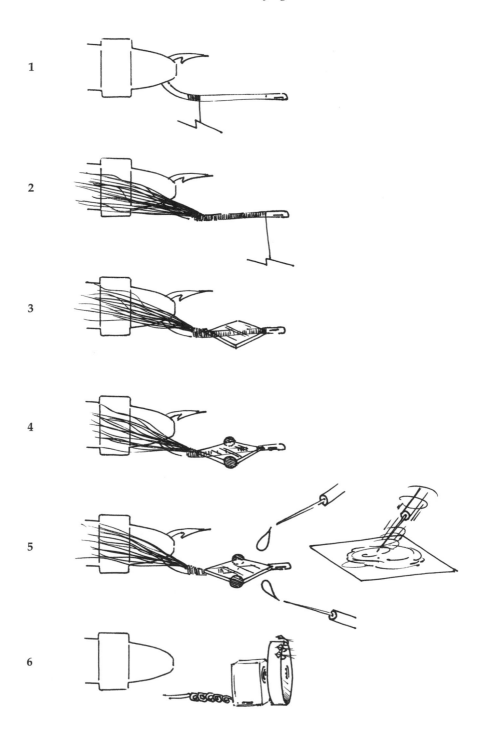

1

2

3

4

5

6

VELVET TUBING EELS

Velvet tubing flies, originated by Brian Owens, are simple to make and ideal for imitating eels and worms. Velvet tubing is available through fly-tying sources and in fabric stores, where it is sold in black, maroon, and white. White is a good color, since it can be dyed or colored with felt-tip markers to suit conditions. These flies can also be made of nylon bolo tubing or parachute cord. Suggested hook sizes: 4 to 1/0.

Step 1. Remove the center strands from a length of velvet or nylon tubing. Choose a piece of velvet tubing up to 5 inches long, and hold it against a hook, one end against the hook eye, to mark the position for hook penetration.

Step 2. Once the hook exit point is chosen, run the hook through the head end of the tubing and out the chosen exit point. Place the hook in a fly-tying vise.

Step 3. Tie in the thread behind the hook eye, then tie down the end of the tubing.

Step 4. With the tubing secured, add eyes. Depending on how deep you plan to fish, eyes can be dumbbell, bead chain, or plastic bead.

Step 5. Once the eyes are crisscrossed in place and held securely, tie off the head of the fly with a whip finish.

Step 6. Finish the fly by cutting the tail at an angle. Seal nylon with a flame. Seal velvet with fabric glue and trim with scissors. Let the glue cure for twenty-four hours before using the fly.

Variations: A thicker head can be built up of chenille or cactus chenille around the eyes. For smaller flies, use the same technique with any hollow tubing cord, such as bolo cord or parachute cord.

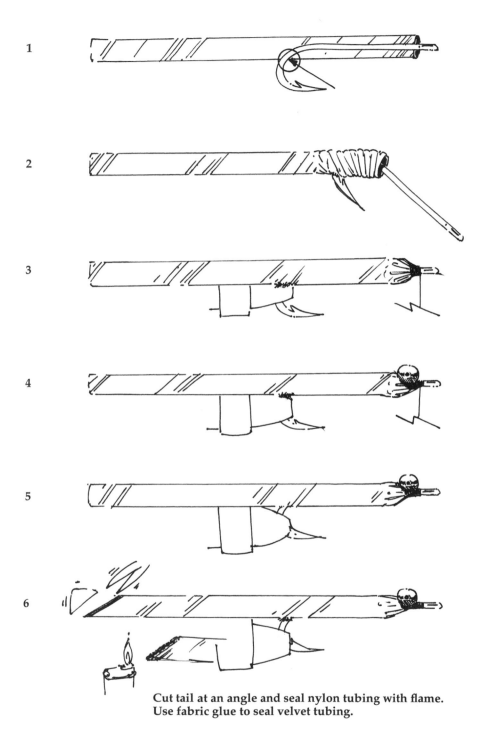

1

2

3

4

5

6

Cut tail at an angle and seal nylon tubing with flame.
Use fabric glue to seal velvet tubing.

'CUDA OR NEEDLEFISH FLIES

Barracuda will take a wide range of flies, but a long, slim needlefish pattern is one of the best, fished fast with a two-handed retrieve. Because of the barracuda's sharp teeth, durable synthetics such as Super Hair, Ultra Hair, FisHair, and similar materials are often best for the long wings. Many patterns and styles of needlefish flies are available. The following is a basic generic style. Suggested hook sizes: 1 to 3/0.

Step 1. Tie in colored thread at the rear of the hook shank.

Step 2. Tie down 4 to 8 inches of white synthetic hair.

Step 3. Tie down a thin layer of light blue synthetic hair on top of the white, followed by a final layer of dark blue synthetic hair.

Step 4. Clip the excess synthetic hair at an angle ahead of the tie-down point.

Step 5. Use the colored thread to completely wrap and cover the wing material on the hook shank and to make a smooth, even, tapered, colored body. Add or paint on eyes if desired.

Step 6. Finish the head and complete with a whip finish, then seal with epoxy. To keep the long wing from flaring in the water and to maintain the slim, needlefishlike appearance, seal the end of the wing with glue or tying wraps.

Variations: You can use a braided ribbing to make a shiny body, and other colors and materials for the wing.

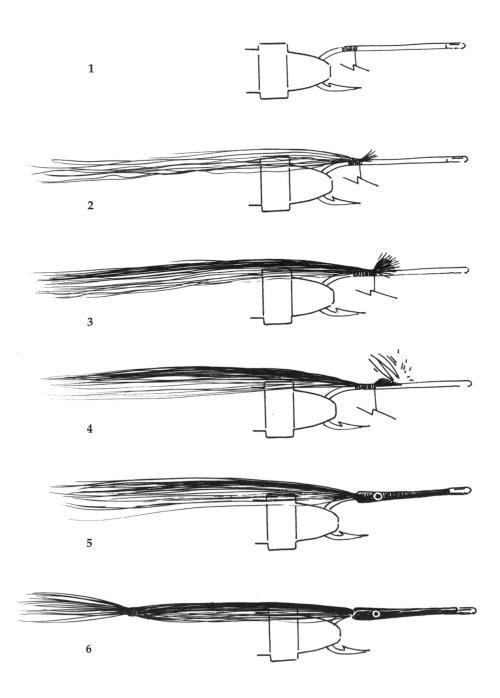

BIG GAME POPPERS AND FLIES

Large flies and poppers are used when offshore fishing for marlin, tuna, and sharks. Poppers or popper heads will make a noise, and the large fly-like tail often attracts hits. Most are used in sight fishing to fish attracted to the boat by trolled teasers. Many styles, sizes, materials, colors, and variations are possible. Many of these are tied in tube versions (see Tube Flies on page 220). The following is a basic generic style. Suggested hook sizes: 2/0 to 7/0.

Step 1. Tie in strong thread at the rear of the hook shank, then tie in a large bundle of saddle hackles or schlappen feathers.

Step 2. Tie in a few strands of flash material, such as Krystal Flash or Flashabou, to each side of this large wing. Clip excess materials.

Step 3. Wrap the thread forward, and then tie in a bundle of shorter hackle, synthetic hair, or natural fur.

Step 4. Add a bundle of dark blue or green natural or synthetic fur or hair to the top of this forward wing as a topping. Clip the excess.

Step 5. Finish the head with thread, then tie off with a whip finish. Glue large doll or plastic eyes to the sides of the formed head.

Step 6. Coat the head and eyes completely with epoxy for protection.

Variations: This fly can be tied without the forward wing, but with a topping on the rear wing and an Ethafoam bug body glued to the forward part of the hook. It can also be tied tandem by first tying a wire or 60- to 100-pound-test mono leader to a hook, then tying on a large rear wing. Then, with the rear hook point-up, secure the leader to the forward hook and finish with a wing wrap as above. Usually there is only an inch or two of leader between the two hooks, with the rear hook one size smaller than the forward hook.

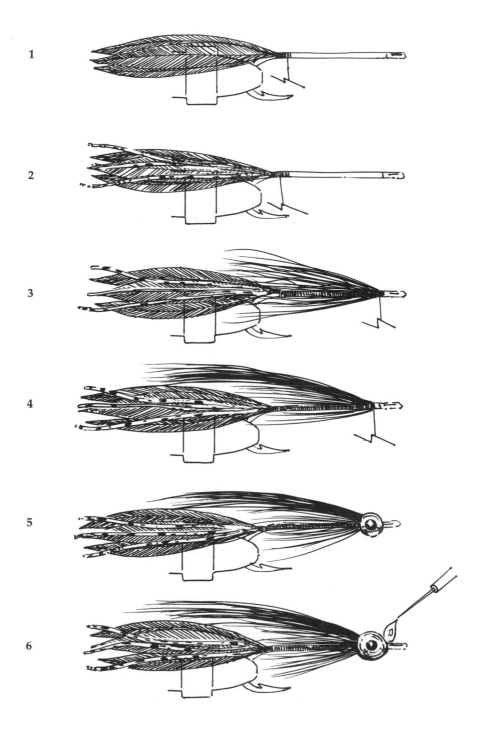

STREAMERS

Saltwater streamers effectively imitate small minnows, shiners, killifish, and other baitfish. They are easy to tie and can be as simple or complex as you like. Often the wings of saltwater streamers are proportionately longer than with freshwater streamers. Streamers can be tied in any size, from 6 through 6/0. The following is a basic generic streamer.

Step 1. Tie in the thread at the head of the hook.

Step 2. Tie in a body material of tinsel or bright synthetic braided material.

Step 3. Wrap this material down the length of the hook shank, then reverse direction and wrap back up the hook shank. Tie off the body material with the thread, and clip the excess.

Step 4. Clip a small bundle of fur, such as bucktail or synthetic. Use a fine-toothed comb to remove the underfur, then hold over the hook shank and tie down as above, with several turns of thread.

Step 5. Clip the excess fur forward of the tie-in point, then completely wrap the rest of the head area with thread.

Step 6. Finish with a whip finish, clip the excess thread, and protect the thread wrap with several coats of head cement or clear nail polish.

Variations: Streamer bodies can be made of multiple materials, wrapping tinsel around a yarn body, for example. Also, streamer wings can be layered of several different colors or materials. Flash materials can be included for added attraction.

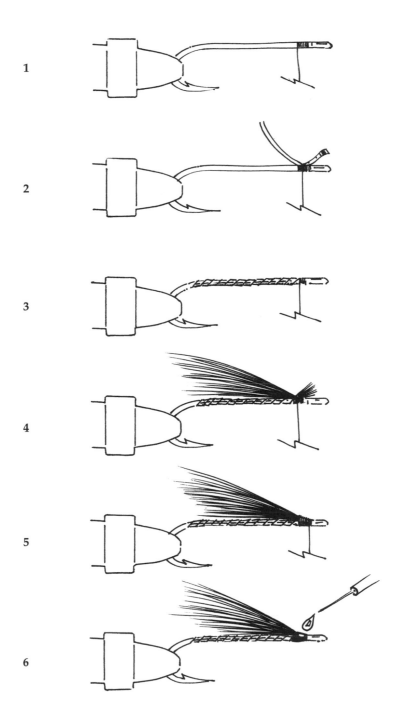

CLOUSER MINNOWS

Developed by Bob Clouser, these flies have proven superior for both fresh and salt water. In essence, they are slim, minnowlike patterns with dumbbell eyes that plummet them to the bottom. With lead eyes on the bottom of the fly as it rides with the hook point-up, it is also very snagproof. They are easy to tie in a variety of color combinations. Suggested hook sizes: 4 to 3/0.

Step 1. Place a long-shank hook in the vise and tie down thread.

Step 2. Tie down lead dumbbell eyes, figure-eighting them with the thread to position them on top of the hook shank.

Step 3. Turn the hook over in the vise so that the hook is point-up and the lead eyes are on the bottom. Tie in a bundle of light-colored bucktail, and trim any excess in front of the wrap.

Step 4. Tie in a small bunch of flash material, such as Flashabou or Krystal Flash.

Step 5. Tie in a bundle of darker bucktail on top to simulate the darker back of most baitfish. Trim excess material.

Step 6. Wrap to form a head, then tie off with a whip finish and seal with head cement or epoxy.

Variations: These can be tied smaller or larger, and the sink rate varied by the size of lead eyes used. Bead chain or other eyes will produce a slower sink rate. Use color combinations to simulate local baitfish.

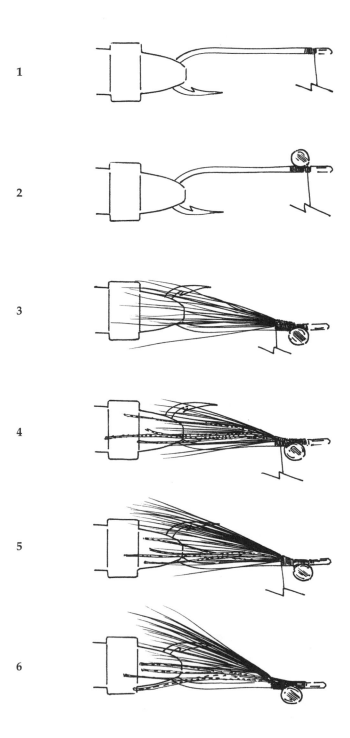

CRAB FLIES

Crab flies are perhaps the best offering for permit, an extremely difficult fish to catch on flies. Many other saltwater species also eat a variety of crab species along all coasts. Most of these flies should be tied small, but different sizes and sink rates are also desirable. Since crabs swim sideways, it is important to tie the flies with the crab positioned sideways on the hook shank. Many patterns are possible, using a variety of different techniques and materials, but the following is a simple version. Suggested hook sizes: 6 to 2/0.

Step 1. Using a regular-shank hook, tie thread in the middle of the hook shank. Tie in burnt mono eyes so that they project out to one side.

Step 2. Tie in a small bundle of Lumaflex, rubber, silicone, or other tough material for legs. These should line up with the hook axis. Tie off with a whip finish.

Step 3. From cloth-backed vinyl (not clear), cut a small carapace-shaped piece that from point to point will be the length of the hook shank. Cut a small, round piece to serve as the abdomen.

Step 4. Using five-minute epoxy, add a small spot of glue to the underside of the carapace, and position the hook on top of it, point-up.

Step 5. Add glue to the abdomen, and position that on top of the hook shank. Use a clamp to hold the parts together (tiny plastic doll clothespins work well for this).

Step 6. Before the glue sets, pull the legs out and flare along each side to resemble crab legs.

Variations: A variation I like for the eyes is to tightly wrap clear, 50- to 100-pound-test mono around a ¼-inch dowel, soak in boiling water, and then quench in cold water. Remove the springlike mono from the dowel, and cut along one side to make a series of round mono "links." Use a lighter to burn both ends. Tie this in the middle of the hook shank, and the eyes automatically extend out to the sides when tied down to line up with the front of the crab.

These flies can also be made to sink by adding lead fuse wire to the hook shank or lead dumbbell eyes just in back of the hook eye.

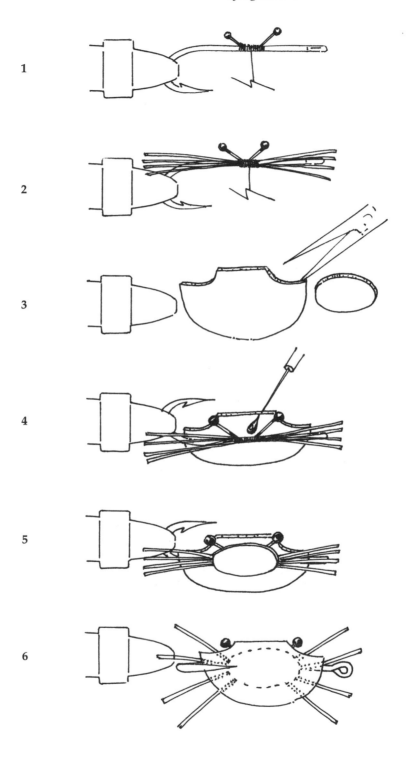

SHRIMP FLIES

Shrimp are taken by game fish worldwide. There are many species of shrimp, and this pattern simulates the basic swimming shrimp, not the snapping shrimp or mantis shrimp, for which there also are patterns. Many swimming shrimp patterns are similarly tied, and this basic design can be varied with different materials and tying techniques. Suggested long-shank hook sizes: 6 to 1/0.

Step 1. Tie the thread to the rear of the hook shank, and then add eyes, such as burnt mono or hair-brush bristle, so that they project in back of the hook bend.

Step 2. Tie in a bundle of Super Hair or Ultra Hair, with the ragged ends extending in back of the eyes and slightly in front of the hook eye.

Step 3. Tie in a length of cactus chenille at the hook bend. Wrap the thread forward to the eye of the hook.

Step 4. Wrap the cactus chenille forward to the hook eye and tie off. Clip excess. Flare the Super Hair down below the hook eye, and trim to resemble a shrimp tail.

Step 5. Cut a carapace for the shrimp from clear or colored transparent vinyl, available at sewing stores. The shape should neck slightly just forward of the tail area and taper toward the front end. Notch the forward end, and keep the total length no longer than the hook shank including eye.

Step 6. Poke a hole in the neck, slide over the hook eye, and wrap at this point. Then spiral-wrap thread forward to make shell segments, and tie off at the rear of the hook shank. Whip-finish and seal with head cement.

Variations: Different colors of transparent vinyl, cactus chenille, and Super Hair can be used. Shrimp in different areas tend to take on the color of their food, so check local samples. The pattern can also be tied with a mono weedguard for fishing in grassy areas, where shrimp often abound.

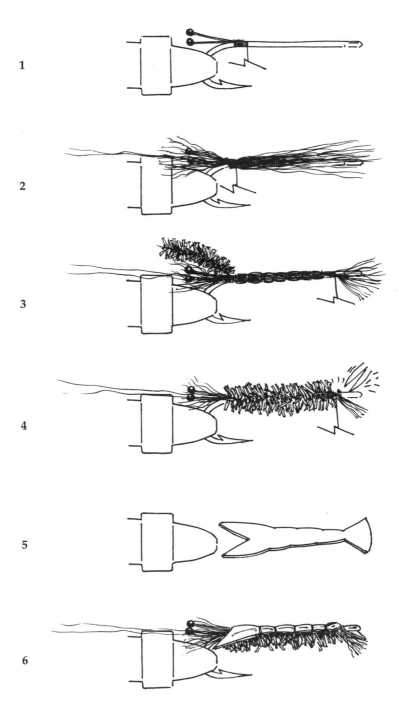

CHUM FLIES

Chum flies are tied to simulate chunks of fish flesh that are used when chumming. Colors should resemble the chum color, which can be white, tan, brown, orange, red, or black. They are not retrieved, but drifted with the chum until hit by the excited fish. Suggested hook sizes: 2 to 2/0, to 5/0 for offshore fishing.

Step 1. Tie the thread to the rear of the hook shank.

Step 2. Tie in a length of cross-cut Zonker rabbit strip of the preferred color.

Step 3. Wrap the thread forward to the hook eye.

Step 4. Spiral the cross-cut Zonker strip forward, and tie down with thread. It helps to slightly wet the rabbit fur to keep it under control while tying. Trim the excess rabbit fur.

Step 5. Complete a head of thread, and tie off with a whip finish.

Step 6. Seal with epoxy or head cement.

Variations: You can include a dense tail of marabou with a short, chunky body of the same color chenille. Cactus chenille is also a possibility. These flies are usually tied unweighted, but for areas with an extremely strong current or tide, lead fuse wire can be added before the other materials to get the fly down to the fish.

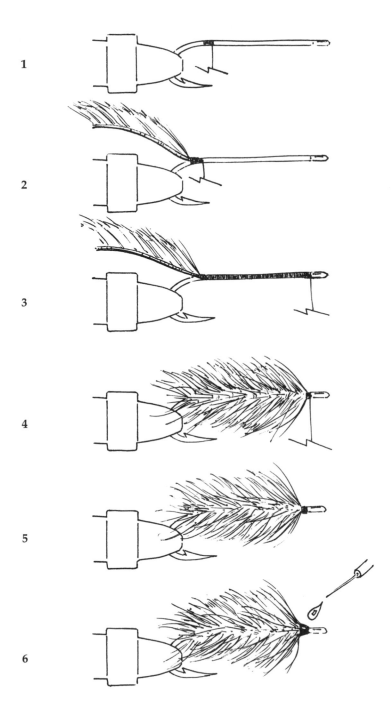

POPPING BUGS

Sliders, poppers, and plain cylinders of closed-cell foam make bug construction easy. Since they are colored and smooth, no painting is required, and they are very effective and durable. Many designs can be made. Suggested hook sizes: 2 to 4/0.

Step 1. Choose a cylinder or body shape for the hook size desired. Use an awl or bodkin to make a hole through the belly side from front to back.

Step 2. Place the hook, preferably kink-shank, in the vise, tie in the thread at the middle of the hook, and tie in a tail of fur, feathers, or synthetics. Wrap securely, then tie in a soft hackle feather.

Step 3. Wrap the hackle feather around the hook shank several times, then tie off with the thread and wrap the thread through the hackle to secure it. Clip excess hackle.

Step 4. Wrap the thread forward on the hook and tie off.

Step 5. Try forcing the hook, eye-first, into the hole made in the foam body. Back out the hook, add some glue to the hook shank, preferably cyanoacrylate glue for regular foam or epoxy for Ethafoam, and slide the hook in place.

Step 6. Immediately adjust the hook position, since cyanoacrylate glue cures rapidly.

Variations: Many colors, sizes, and styles of bugs are possible using this simple basic technique. Bugs with cork and balsa bodies are made the same way but require shaping then gluing the body to the hook, and then painting it. Many saltwater poppers are tied without a hackle collar.

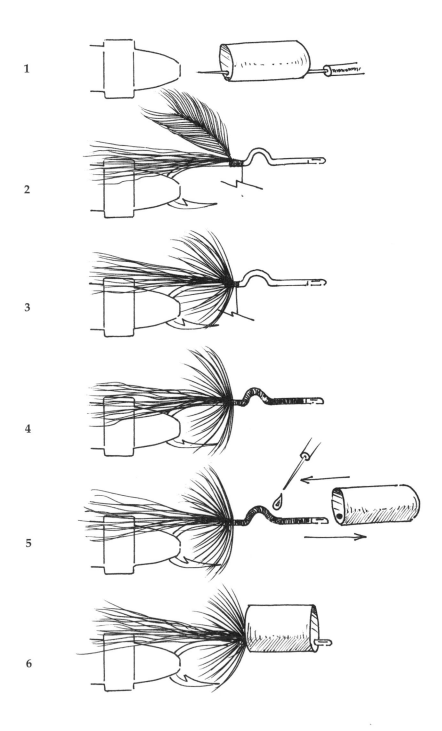

TOOTHY CRITTER FLIES

Many saltwater fish have teeth. Barracuda, bluefish, snappers, and sharks are prime examples, but others also have smaller teeth that, in big fish, can still easily cut a mono leader. Simple flies for these fish use a long-shank stainless steel hook. Some of these are not designed for fly tying; carefully and safely bend straight any kirbed or offset bend. By tying on the rear of the hook, the forward hook shank serves as a very tough "mini leader." In some cases, it is also helpful to add another few inches of single-strand wire attached with a haywire twist. This one I developed for bluefish, but it can be used for any toothy fish. Suggested hook sizes: 2 to 4/0.

Step 1. If using a long-shank hook with a kirbed or offset hook, straighten with pliers. Place in the vise.

Step 2. Tie on thread at the very rear of the hook shank.

Step 3. Tie down a bundle of light-colored natural bucktail or synthetic wing material. Clip off the excess forward of the wrap.

Step 4. Tie a bundle of darker wing material on top of the light-colored wing.

Step 5. Tie a few strands of flash material to each side of this wing. Clip off all excess wing material.

Step 6. Finish the head with thread wraps, then tie off with a whip finish. Coat with epoxy to protect from teeth. Leave the forward part of the hook shank bare.

Variations: Any color combination of wing material can be used. Synthetics are best for their durability. You can also use stranded materials for the tail, dividing into three bundles, plaiting the result, and tying off at the end.

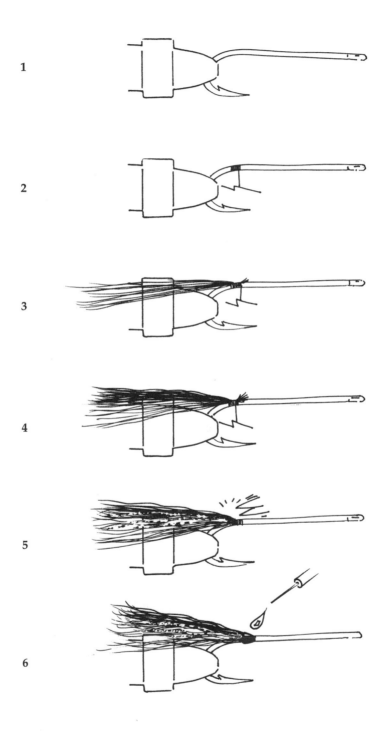

THE INVINCIBLE

I developed the Invincible as a large, baitfishlike fly for pike, but it is also excellent for any toothy fish and as is indestructible as a fly can be, since all wrapped parts are protected by epoxy. As with many flies used in salt water, it can be tied in any size, color, and tail length. Synthetics such as Super Hair, Ultra Hair, Neer Hair, Aqua Fiber, or Bozo Hair are a must for the tail. Use Body Fur for the body. Suggested hook sizes: 6 to 5/0.

Step 1. Clamp a long-shank hook in the vise, and tie down the thread along the length of the shank.

Step 2. Tie in one or several colors of long-stranded synthetics (Super Hair is ideal), along with a little stranded flash material on each side.

Step 3. Tie down one end of a length of Body Fur. Mix some five-minute epoxy, and coat the hook shank and thread wraps holding the tail and Body Fur in place.

Step 4. Palmer the Body Fur forward to the head, making sure that each turn is in the wet epoxy base.

Step 5. Tie off at the head, clip the excess material, tie off with a whip finish, and stick prism eyes to the head.

Step 6. Using the remainder of the epoxy, seal the eyes and head of the fly, placing the fly on a rotator to cure.

Variations: The fly can be tied with a mono weedguard for fishing around weeds and structure. Also, light-colored flies can be colored in the field with permanent felt-tip markers to mark back countershading, vertical bars, and spots.

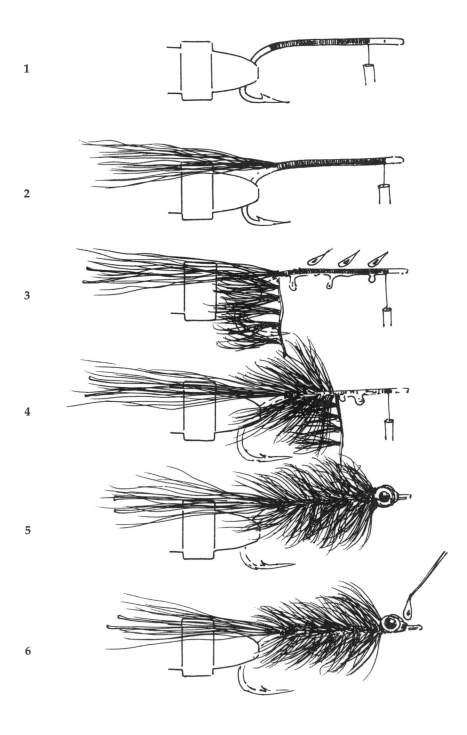

BENDBACK OR KEEL-STYLE FLIES

With slight modifications, almost any fly can be tied on bendback or keel hooks. These hooks are different, but both are designed to ride point-up, with the wing protecting or covering the hook point. Keel hook flies are almost always tied with a body; bendback styles are tied with or without a body.

With keel hooks, the fly is positioned in the vise point-up, with any tail, body, and ribbing tied in place, ending up at the eye of the hook. Then a wing, of one or more materials, is tied and wrapped in place and the head finished. With keel hook flies, the wing will extend straight back from the shank immediately in back of the hook eye to line up with and cover the hook point.

Bendback hooks have only a single bend near the eye. In some cases, a body is tied in place, as with keel hooks; in others, only a wing is tied on and the shank left bare. Some fishermen, such as bass anglers, also use offset-shank worm hooks to accomplish the same thing. Suggested hook sizes: 6 to 4/0.

On keel hook

Bottomfish flies

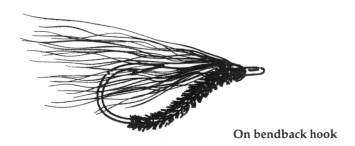

On bendback hook

TUBE FLIES

Almost all flies can be tied as tube flies. Tube flies are not tied on hooks, but on lengths of thin, plastic or plastic-lined metal tubing through which the leader is run and then tied to a hook. In some cases, a soft, vinyl tubing is added at the tail of the fly to hold the eye of the hook. Another way to keep the hook or sections of tubes in position is to use a bobber stop in front of the tube, the stop slid tight against the tube.

Special tube-fly vises are available to hold tubes of different sizes, with the wrapping and tying techniques otherwise almost identical to tying on hooks. Tube poppers, in which a tube is glued into a foam popper body, are also popular, especially for big game fishing, where they are added in front of flies for flotation and noise.

Step 1. Place the tube on the pin of the tube-fly vise, tie in the thread at the rear, and tie down a piece of cactus chenille.

Step 2. Wrap the thread forward, followed by the chenille. Tie off.

Step 3. Tie in a bundle of craft fur, synthetic fur, or natural fur with two or three loose wraps of thread.

Step 4. Push down on the fur wing with your thumb to spread the fibers completely around the tube.

Step 5. Finish wrapping the head, and then whip-finish and clip excess thread.

Step 6. Protect the finished wrap with a coating of head cement or epoxy.

Variations: Almost any pattern or type of fly can be tied on a tube. In addition, modular parts of flies can be tied on short tubes, combining the appropriate sections of wing, body, head, and eyes to make the required fly for each fishing situation.

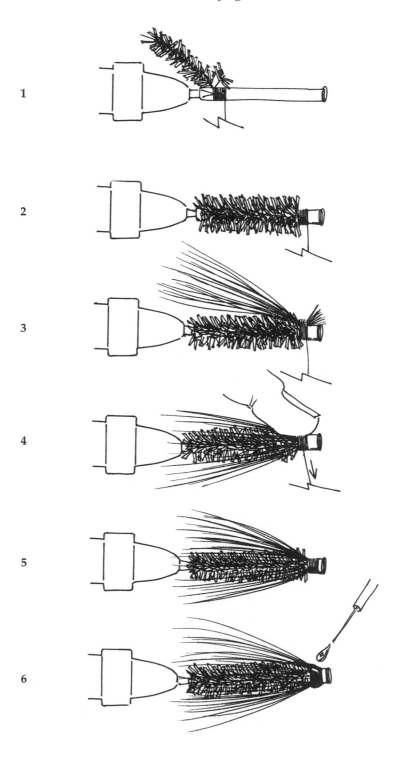

Finally

Enjoy saltwater fly fishing. Don't take it too seriously. Have fun—that's what it's all about. Take the sport seriously enough to be successful, but casually enough to enjoy it all. Learn the basics—good casting; choice of flies; techniques for different waters, different structure, and different fish; fishing patterns; and methods for different times of the year. Most important, learn about the fish you seek—their habits and habitat—to know where, when, and how to cast that fly. Do that, and you'll hook as much out of this sport as you put into it—and more.

Bibliography

FLY FISHING

Abrames, Kenney. *Striper Moon—Fly Fishing Techniques and Flies for Striped Bass in Estuary, River, Bay and Surf.* Portland, OR: Frank Amato Publications, 1994.

Beck, Barry and Cathy. *Fly-Fishing the Flats.* Mechanicsburg, PA: Stackpole Books, 1999.

Bondorew, Ray. *Stripers and Streamers.* Portland, OR: Frank Amato Publications, 1996.

Brown, Dick. *Fly Fishing for Bonefish.* New York: The Lyons Press, 1993.

Bruce, Joe. *Fly Fishing for Striped Bass.* Woodbine, MD: K & D Ltd., 1997.

Combs, Trey. *Bluewater Fly Fishing.* New York: The Lyons Press, 1995.

Crawford, Jim. *Salmon to a Fly: Fly Fishing for Pacific Salmon in the Open Ocean.* Portland, OR: Frank Amato Publications, 1995.

Curcione, Nick. *Baja on the Fly.* Portland, OR: Frank Amato Publications, 1998.

———. *The Orvis Guide to Saltwater Fly Fishing.* New York: The Lyons Press, 1993.

Currier, Jeff. *Currier's Quick and Easy Guide to Saltwater Fly Fishing.* Helena, MT: Greycliff Publishing Company, 1998.

Earnhardt, Tom. *Fly Fishing the Tidewaters.* New York: The Lyons Press, 1995.

Ferguson, Bruce, Les Johnson, and Pat Trotter. *Fly Fishing for Pacific Salmon.* Portland, OR: Frank Amato Publications, 1985.

Hughes, Dave. *Fly Fishing Basics.* Mechanicsburg, PA: Stackpole Books, 1994.

Kaufmann, Randall. *Bonefishing with a Fly.* Portland, OR: Frank Amato Publications, 1992.

Kreh, Lefty. *Fly Fishing in Salt Water.* New York: The Lyons Press, 1997.

Kumiski, Capt. John A. *Fishing the Everglades—A Complete Guide for the Small Boater.* Maitland, FL: Argonaut Publishing, 1993.

————. *Flyfishing for Redfish.* Maitland, FL: Argonaut Publishing, 1997.

————. *Flyrodding Florida Salt.* Maitland, FL: Argonaut Publishing, 1995.

————. *Saltwater Fly Fishing.* Point Pleasant, NJ: The Fisherman Library, 1994.

LaFontaine, Gary, and Ron Cordes. *Pocket Guide to Saltwater Fly Fishing.* Helena, MT: Greycliff Publishing Company, 1994.

Mitchell, Ed. *Fly Rodding the Coast.* Mechanicsburg, PA: Stackpole Books, 1995.

Preble, Capt. Dave. *Fly Fishing Offshore: Cape Cod to Cape Hatteras.* Point Pleasant, NJ: The Fisherman Library, 1998.

Raychard, Al. *Bonefish, Tarpon, Permit, Fly Fishing Guide—The Big Three.* Portland, OR: Frank Amato Publications, 1996.

————. *Fly Fishing the Salt.* Unity, ME: North Country Press, 1989.

Raymond, Steve. *The Estuary Flyfisher.* Portland, OR: Frank Amato Publications, 1996.

Reynolds, John. *Flyfishing for Sailfish.* Machynlleth, Powys, Wales: Coch-y-Bonddu Books, 1997.

Samson, Jack. *Billfish on a Fly.* Portland, OR: Frank Amato Publications, 1995.

————. *Permit on a Fly.* Mechanicsburg, PA: Stackpole Books, 1996.

————. *Saltwater Fly Fishing.* Mechanicsburg, PA: Stackpole Books, 1991.

Sosin, Mark, and Lefty Kreh. *Fishing the Flats.* New York: The Lyons Press, 1983.

Swisher, Doug, and Carl Richards. *Backcountry Fly Fishing in Salt Water.* New York: The Lyons Press, 1995.

Tabory, Lou. *Inshore Fly Fishing.* New York: The Lyons Press, 1992.

FLY CASTING

Jaworowski, Ed. *The Cast.* Mechanicsburg, PA: Stackpole Books, 1992.

Kreh, Lefty. *Longer Fly Casting.* New York: The Lyons Press, 1991.

Lewis, Gary, Marnie Reed Crowell, and Peter H. McNair. *Fly Casting for Everyone.* Mechanicsburg, PA: Stackpole Books, 1996.

Schollmeyer, Jim, and Frank Amato. *Fly Casting Illustrated in Color.* Portland, OR: Frank Amato Publications, 1993.

Wulff, Joan. *Joan Wulff's Fly Casting Techniques.* New York: The Lyons Press, 1987.

FLY TYING

Brown, Dick. *Bonefish Fly Patterns.* New York: The Lyons Press, 1996.

Caolo, Alan. *Fly Fisherman's Guide to Atlantic Baitfish & Other Food Sources.* Portland, OR: Frank Amato Publications, 1995.

Fitzgerald, f-stop. *Secrets of the Saltwater Fly.* Boston: Bullfinch Press, 1996.

Gartside, Jack. *Striper Flies.* Privately printed, 1995.

Kreh, Lefty. *Saltwater Fly Patterns.* New York: The Lyons Press, 1995.

Mandell, Mark, and Les Johnson. *Tube Flies—A Tying, Fishing & Historical Guide.* Portland, OR: Frank Amato Publications, 1995.

Meyer, Deke. *Saltwater Flies: Over 700 of the Best.* Portland, OR: Frank Amato Publications, 1995.

———. *Tying Saltwater Flies: 12 of the Best.* Portland, OR: Frank Amato Publications, 1996.

Pfeiffer, C. Boyd. *Bug Making.* New York: Lyons Press, 1993.

Richards, Carl. *Prey.* New York: The Lyons Press, 1995.

Roberts, George V. *A Fly-Fisher's Guide to Saltwater Naturals and Their Imitation.* Camden, ME: Ragged Mountain Press, 1994.

Stewart, Dick, and Farrow Allen. *Flies for Saltwater.* North Conway, NH: Northland Press, 1992.

Tabory, Lou. *Lou Tabory's Guide to Saltwater Baits & Their Imitations.* New York: The Lyons Press, 1995.

Talleur, Dick. *Talleur's Basic Fly Tying.* New York: The Lyons Press, 1996.

Van Vliet, John. *The Art of Fly Tying.* Minnetonka, MN: Cy DeCosse, 1994.

Veverka, Bob. *Innovative Saltwater Flies.* Mechanicsburg, PA: Stackpole Books, 1999.

Wentink, Frank. *Saltwater Fly Tying.* New York: The Lyons Press, 1991.

Wilson, Donald. *Smelt Fly Patterns.* Portland, OR: Frank Amato Publications, 1996.

SPECIES AND GENERAL REFERENCE

These are not fly-fishing books per se, but do contain vital information about species and their habitats.

Barrett, Capt. Pete. *Fishing for Sharks.* Point Pleasant, NJ: The Fisherman Library, 1997.

———. *Fishing for Tuna and Marlin.* Point Pleasant, NJ: The Fisherman Library, 1992.

Caputi, Gary. *Fishing for Striped Bass.* Point Pleasant, NJ: The Fisherman Library, 1993.

Genova, Phil. *First Cast.* Mechanicsburg, PA: Stackpole Books, 1998.

Kamienski, Don. *Fishing for Fluke.* Point Pleasant, NJ: The Fisherman Library, 1993.

Karas, Nick. *The Striped Bass.* New York: The Lyons Press, 1993.

Pfeiffer, C. Boyd. *Shad Fishing.* New York: Crown Publishers, 1976.

Ristori, Capt. Al. *Fishing for Bluefish.* Point Pleasant, NJ: The Fisherman Library, 1995.

———. *The Saltwater Fish Identifier.* New York: Mallard Press, 1992.

Sargeant, Frank. *The Masters Book of Snook.* Lakeland, FL: Larsen's Outdoor Publishing, 1997.

————. *The Redfish Book.* Lakeland, FL: Larsen's Outdoor Publishing, 1991.

————. *The Reef Fishing Book.* Lakeland, FL: Larsen's Outdoor Publishing, 1996.

————. *The Snook Book.* Lakeland, FL: Larsen's Outdoor Publishing, 1991.

————. *The Tarpon Book.* Lakeland, FL: Larsen's Outdoor Publishing, 1991.

————. *The Trout Book.* Lakeland, FL: Larsen's Outdoor Publishing, 1992.

Schaffner, Herbert A. *Saltwater Game Fish.* New York: Gallery Books, 1989.

Soucie, Gary. *Hook, Line and Sinker.* New York: The Lyons Press, 1982.

————. *Soucie's Fishing Databook.* New York: The Lyons Press, 1985.

Walters, Keith. *Chesapeake Stripers.* Bozman, MD: Aerie House, 1990.

Woolner, Frank and Henry Lyman. *Striped Bass Fishing.* New York: The Lyons Press, 1995.

MAGAZINES AND PERIODICALS

Black's Fly Fishing, 43 W. Front St., Suite 11, Red Bank, NJ 07701. Annual reference publication on equipment, instruction, and destinations.

Fly Fish America, P.O. Box 408, Fryeburg, ME 04037. Available at fly shops. Several regional editions.

Fly Fisherman, Primedia Special Interest Publications, 6405 Flank Dr., Harrisburg, PA 17112. Covers all types of fly fishing.

Fly Fishing Worldwide, Ocean Arts, Inc., 9121 SW 103rd Ave., Miami, FL 33176-1609. Newsletter for traveling fly anglers.

Fly Fishing in Salt Waters, Hook and Release Publishing, Inc., 2001 Western Ave., #210, Seattle, WA 98121. Specifically about saltwater fishing.

Fly Rod & Reel, Down East Enterprises, Roxmont, Rte. 1, Rockport, ME 04856. Covers all types of fly fishing.

Fly Tyer, Abenaki Publishers, Inc., P.O. Box 4100, Bennington, VT 05201. Covers all types of fly tying.

Fly Tying, Frank Amato Publications, P.O. Box 82112, Portland, OR 97282. Covers all types of fly tying.

The Fly Fisher, Keokee Co. Publishing, P.O. Box 722, Sandpoint, ID 83864. General fly fishing.

The Inside Angler, P.O. Box 31282, San Francisco, CA 94131-0282. General fishing destination newsletter.

The Panangler, 180 N. Michigan Ave., Chicago, IL 60601. International fishing destination newsletter.

Saltwater Fly Fishing, Abenaki Publishers, Inc., P.O. Box 4100, Bennington, VT 05201. Specifically about saltwater fly fishing and fly tying.

Western Flyfishing, Frank Amato Publications, P.O. Box 82112, Portland, OR 97282. Western fly fishing, both fresh and salt water.

Index